OUTCASTS UNITED

OUTCASTS UNITED

The Story of a
Refugee Soccer Team
That Changed a Town

WARREN ST. JOHN

DELACORTE PRESS

All rights reserved. Published in the United States by Delacorte Press, an
imprint of Random House Children's Books, a division of Random House,
Inc., New York. This work is based on *Outcasts United,* copyright © 2009
by Warren St. John, published in hardcover by Spiegel & Grau,
a division of the Random House Group.

Delacorte Press is a registered trademark and the colophon is
a trademark of Random House, Inc.

Visit us on the Web! randomhouse.com/teens
Educators and librarians, for a variety of teaching tools, visit us at
RHTeachersLibrarians.com

Library of Congress Cataloging-in-Publication Data
St. John, Warren.
    Outcasts united : the story of a refugee soccer team that changed a town /
Warren St. John.
        p. cm.
    ISBN 978-0-385-74194-1 (trade hc) — ISBN 978-0-375-99033-5
(glb hc) — ISBN 978-0-375-98880-6 (ebook)
    1. Mufleh, Luma. 2. Soccer coaches—Georgia—Clarkston—Biography.
3. Refugee children—Georgia—Clarkston. 4. Refugees—Africa.   I. Title.
    GV942.7.L86 2012   796.334092—dc23   [B]   2012001412

The text of this book is set in 11.5-point Adobe Caslon.
Book design by Vikki Sheatsley

Printed in the United States of America
10 9 8 7 6 5 4 3 2 1
First Edition

Random House Children's Books supports the First Amendment
and celebrates the right to read.

For Alex, Bienvenue,
Ive, and Alyah

CONTENTS

OUTCASTS
UNITED

INTRODUCTION

On a cool spring afternoon on a soccer field in northern Georgia, two teams of teenage boys were going through their pregame warm-ups. The field was quiet except for the thumping of soccer balls against forefeet and the rustling of the balls against the nylon nets hanging from the goals. Suddenly, there was a rumble. As it grew louder, all motion stopped, and boys from both teams looked skyward. Above was a squadron of fighter jets on their way to an air show miles away in Atlanta. The aircraft came closer, so that the boys could make out the markings on the wings and the white helmets of the pilots in the cockpits. Then, with a roar loud enough to rattle the change in a person's pockets, the jets shot off in different directions like an exploding firework.

The teams watched with craned necks. The players on the

home team—a group of thirteen- and fourteen-year-old boys from the nearby Atlanta suburbs playing with the North Atlanta Soccer Association—gestured toward the sky with awe. The boys at the other end of the field were members of an all-refugee soccer team called the Fugees. Many had actually seen fighter jets in action, and all had felt the results of war firsthand. There were Sudanese players on the team whose villages had been bombed, and Liberians who'd lived through mortar fire that pierced the roofs of their neighbors' homes, taking out whole families. As the jets flew over the field, several members of the Fugees flinched.

"You guys need to concentrate!" a voice interrupted as the jets streaked into the distance.

The voice belonged to Luma Mufleh, the thirty-one-year-old founder and volunteer coach of the Fugees. Her players resumed their practice shots, but they seemed distracted. Their shots flew hopelessly over the goal.

"If you shoot like that, you're going to lose," Coach Luma said.

Luma shouted to her players to gather around her. She gave them their positions and they took the field. Forty or so parents had gathered on the home team's sideline to cheer their boys on, and they clapped as their sons walked onto the pitch. There was no one on the Fugees' sideline. Most of the players came from single-parent families, and their mothers or fathers—usually mothers—stayed home on weekends to look after their other children, or else worked, because weekend shifts paid more than weekday shifts. Few had cars to allow them to travel to soccer games. Even at their home games, the Fugees rarely had anyone to cheer them on.

The referee summoned the Fugees to the line to go over their roster and to check their cleats and numbers. Luma handed him the roster, and the referee wrinkled his brow.

"If I mispronounce your name, I apologize," he said. He read through the list. When he got hung up, the boys would politely say their own names, then step forward to declare their jersey numbers.

A few minutes later, a whistle sounded and the game began. The head coach of the North Atlanta team liked to scream. From the outset, he ran back and forth on his sideline, barking at his players in a hoarse bellow: "Man on! Man on! Drop it! Drop it! Turn! Turn! Turn!"

Luma paced silently on her side of the field with an annoyed look on her face. She was all for teaching, but her method was to teach during practice and during the breaks in play. Once the whistle blew, she allowed her players to be themselves: to screw up, to take chances. All the shouting was wearing on her nerves. When North Atlanta scored first, on a free kick, the team's coach jumped up and down, while across the field, parents leaped from their folding lawn chairs in celebration. Luma pursed her lips in a tiny sign of disgust and kept pacing, quietly. A few moments later, Christian Jackson of the Fugees shook himself free on the right side, dribbled downfield, and fired a line drive into the top right corner of the net: goal. Luma betrayed no reaction other than to adjust her tattered white Smith College baseball cap. She continued to pace.

The Fugees soon controlled the ball again, making crisp

passes and moving within range of the goal. A Fugees forward struggled free of traffic to take a shot that flew a good twenty feet over the crossbar and into the parking lot behind the field. Luma paced.

Meanwhile, with each of his team's shots, the North Atlanta coach shouted more commands. He was getting upset. He obviously believed that if his players had done as he said, they could've scored on Manchester United. But as it was, they ended the first half trailing the Fugees 3–1.

A 3–1 lead at halftime would have pleased most soccer coaches. But Luma was not pleased. Her head down, she marched angrily to a corner of the field, the Fugees following. They could tell she was unhappy. They knew what was coming. Luma ordered them to sit down.

"Our team has taken nine shots and made three—they've taken two shots and made one," she told the boys, her voice sharp. "You're outrunning them, outhustling them, outplaying them—why are you only winning three to one?

. "Christian," she said, looking at the boy, who sat on the grass with his arms around his knees. "This is one of your worst games. I want it to be one of your best games. I want to sit back and watch good soccer—do you understand?"

At that moment, the voice of the North Atlanta coach—still screaming at his players—drifted down the field to the Fugees' huddle. Luma turned her gaze toward the source of the offending noise.

"See that coach?" she said. "I want him to sit down and be quiet. That's when you know we've won—when he sits down and shuts up. Got it?"

"Yes, Coach," her players replied.

When the Fugees took the field for the second half, they had changed. They quickly scored three goals. The first, an elegant cross, was chested in by a Sudanese forward named Attak. That was followed by a cannon shot from Christian ten yards out. Moments later, Christian dribbled into the box and faked to his left, a move that left the North Atlanta goalie tangled in his own limbs, before shooting right: another goal. The opposing coach was still yelling—"Man on! Man on!"—so the Fugees kept shooting. Another goal. And another. When the angry North Atlanta players started hacking away at the Fugees' shins and ankles, the Fugees brushed them off and scored yet again.

At 8–2, the North Atlanta coach, hoarse now, wiped the sweat from his forehead with the back of his hand, quietly wandered over to his bench, and sat down. The Fugees tried to stifle their smiles.

If Luma was satisfied, it was hard to tell. She remained perfectly stone-faced. The referee blew his whistle three times to signal the end of the game.

The final score was 9–2 Fugees. Christian Jackson had scored five goals. The teams shook hands and the Fugees quickly ran to the bench for water and oranges, which awaited them in two white plastic grocery bags. A few moments later, the referee approached. He looked to be in his late fifties, white, with a gray mustache. He asked Luma if he could say something to her players. Luma didn't like handing over her team's attention to anyone, especially not to a stranger. But she got her team together in front of the referee some ten yards from their bench.

"Gentlemen," he said, "I'd like to thank you. You played

the ball the entire game, and you didn't take any cheap shots. They got frustrated and started hacking, and you didn't re- taliate. So I'd like to commend you on your sportsmanship." The man paused and swallowed hard. "And that was one of the most beautiful games of soccer I've ever seen."

This was the first time I'd ever seen the Fugees play. I'd shown up as a reporter knowing little about the team other than that it was based in a town called Clarkston, the players were refu- gees, and the coach was a woman.

I'd learned that in a little more than a decade, Clarkston had become one of the most diverse communities in Amer- ica. And yet few in Atlanta, let alone in the world beyond, had noticed.

I came away from that first game wanting to learn more. I had just seen a group of boys from a dozen war-torn coun- tries come together as a team and play beautiful soccer. How? Their coach, an intense and quiet presence who hid beneath the brim of her cap and came out only to give bits of inspira- tion or wisdom, presented another mystery. There was a sense of trust and friendship between the players and their coach, but there was also tension and long silences.

In fact, things with the Fugees were more fragile than I could have realized that day. The team had no home field. The players' private lives were an intense daily struggle to stay afloat. They and their families had fled violence and chaos and found themselves in a place with a completely different set of values and customs.

Luma was struggling too, to hold her team—and herself— together. She had volunteered to help these boys on the field and off, not realizing how great some of their difficulties were: post-traumatic stress, poverty, parental neglect, grief, shattered confidence, and, in more than one case, simple anger at having to live the way they did. Luma, I would learn, had no background in social or human-rights work. She was just a woman who wanted, in her own way, to make the world a better place. She had vowed to come through for her players and their families or to come apart trying.

But more than anything that day, it was the surprising friendship of these kids from different cultures, religions, and backgrounds that drew me into their story. One moment in the game underscored this for me more than any other.

There was a player on the Fugees who was not as good at soccer as his teammates—a tiny defender from Afghanistan named Zubaid. He might have had trouble seeing items close up. When the soccer ball rolled his way, he would draw his foot back, swing his leg with all his might, and usually miss the ball. After this happened a third or fourth time, I asked Luma what the boy's story was. Luma didn't seem the least bit offended. In fact, she seemed proud that Zubaid was on the field. He had never missed a practice or one of the afternoon tutoring sessions Luma made her players attend, she explained. He was on the field because he deserved to be.

When the ball rolled Zubaid's way, his teammates never tried to take it from him, though they were faster and more agile than he was. Instead, two or three members of the Fugees would drop in five or so yards behind him, to form a safe area between Zubaid and the goal. When he missed the ball, they were there to cover for him, but always quietly, and with respect for his effort.

Late in the game, one of the North Atlanta forwards got

loose with the ball on Zubaid's side of the pitch, and Zubaid rushed upfield to defend. He put out his leg, and the ball locked between the tops of the two players' feet with a loud thwump. The ball stopped, and the North Atlanta player fell forward onto the turf: a perfect tackle. Much to his surprise, Zubaid found himself alone, still standing and with possession of the ball, which he quickly passed to a teammate at midfield. At the next lull, when the ball went out of bounds, Zubaid was set upon by his teammates as though he'd scored the winning goal.

Outcasts United is the inspiring true story of this amazing group of boys and their coach.

PART ONE

Changes

1

Luma

The name Luma means "dark lips," though Hassan and Sawsan al-Mufleh chose it for their first child less because of the shade of her lips than because they liked the sound of the name. The al-Muflehs were a wealthy family in Amman, Jordan, a city of two million, set among nineteen hills and cooled by dry desert breezes. The family earned its fortune manufacturing rebar—the metal rods used to strengthen concrete—which it sold across Jordan.

Luma took after her father, Hassan, a man who seemed to keep his emotions hidden for fear of revealing weakness.

"My sister and my dad don't like people going into them and knowing who they are," said Inam al-Mufleh, Luma's younger sister by eleven years, now a researcher for the Jordanian army in Amman. "Luma's very sensitive but she never shows it. She doesn't want anyone to know where her soft spot is."

Hassan doted on his eldest child. He expected her to marry, to stay close to home, and to honor her family. Yet from the time Luma was just a young girl, adults around her began to note a quiet confidence, even independence. But the family also knew another side of Luma—that of a sensitive young woman with a deep concern for the weak or defenseless.

The al-Muflehs sent Luma to the American Community School (ACS) in Amman, a school for the children of American expatriates, mostly diplomats and businessmen, and elite Jordanians, including the children of King Hussein and Queen Noor. Luma learned to speak English without an accent and met kids from the United States and Europe, as well as the children of diplomats from all over the world.

Luma lived at a comfortable distance from Amman's problems, which included poverty and the tensions brought on by the arrival of Palestinian and, later, Iraqi refugees. But her maternal grandmother, Munawar, made a point of helping the poor whenever she could. Beggars regularly knocked on her door because they knew she would always help them.

Munawar's home was near a lot where young men played soccer in the afternoons. As a kid, Luma would climb a grapevine on the concrete wall behind the house and watch the men play. She eventually got the nerve to join in, and she would play until her grandmother saw her and ordered her inside, on the grounds that it was improper for a young girl to be around strange men.

"She would have a fit if she saw me playing soccer with men," Luma said. "And then she'd say, 'We are not going to tell your father about this.'"

At the American Community School, Luma was free to play sports as boys did. She played basketball, volleyball, soccer, and baseball, and stood out to her coaches, particularly an African American woman named Rhonda Brown, who coached volleyball.

"She was keen to learn," Brown said. "And no matter what you asked her to do, she did it without questioning why."

Coach Brown asked a lot of her players, especially of Luma. She expected them to be on time to practice, to work hard, to focus, and to improve. She believed in running—lots of running—and drilling until the players were exhausted. Brown challenged her players by setting an example. She was always on time. She was organized. When she asked her players to run five kilometers, she joined them, but with a challenge: "Because you're younger, I expect you to do it better than me," she told them. "If I beat you, you can expect the worst practices ever."

"They ran," Brown said.

Brown accepted that her players might not like her at first. But she was willing to wait out the hostility in the hope that her players would eventually buy in.

Luma didn't like Brown at all. She felt singled out for extra work and didn't appreciate all the additional running her coach made her do. But she didn't complain.

"I knew my teammates were lazy—talented but lazy," Luma said. "And part of me was like, *Maybe I want the challenge. Maybe these very harsh, very tough practices will work.*"

Over time, the practices began to have an effect. The team improved. They were motivated, and even the slackers began working hard. Luma started to realize that although she told herself she disliked Coach Brown, she wanted very badly to play well for her. "For the majority of the time she coached me, I hated her," Luma said. "But she had our respect. She didn't ask us to do anything she wouldn't do. Until then I'd always played for me. I'd never played for a coach."

As Luma got older and grew accustomed to the liberty she had as a woman at ACS—where she could play sports as she pleased—she began to feel at odds with the strict Jordanian society in which she had grown up. She wanted to be able to play pickup games of soccer with whoever was around, whether they were boys or girls. She wanted to be as strong in her daily life as Coach Brown had taught her to be on the court. Her family's social status, however, meant that she was expected to follow a more traditional path.

Toward the end of Luma's junior year, she and her parents decided she would attend college in the United States. Her father, Hassan, and her mother, Sawsan, wanted her to continue her Western education. But Luma was more interested in life in the United States than she was in what an education there might do for her in Jordan. "America was the land of opportunity," she said. "It was a very appealing dream of what you want your life to be like."

Luma enrolled at Hobart and William Smith College, a coed school in the Finger Lakes region of New York. She played soccer her first fall there, but midway through the season she injured her knee.

Luma liked the school well enough, but winter in upstate New York was colder than anything she had experienced in

Amman, so she decided to look at other schools. She visited Smith College, the all-women's school in Northampton, Massachusetts.

Smith is located in a pretty New England town with a strong sense of community and security. And as a women's college, Smith focuses on giving its students the sort of encouragement to be independent Luma felt she had been deprived of at home. Luma fell in love with the place and transferred for her sophomore year.

Friends from Smith remember Luma as outgoing and involved, active in intramural soccer and in social events sponsored by the college's house system. Few people were aware of her nationality; she spoke English so well that other students assumed she was American.

"One day we were hanging out talking about our childhoods and Luma said, 'I'm from Jordan,'" recalled Misty Wyman, a student from Maine who would become Luma's best friend. "I thought she'd been born to American parents overseas. It had never occurred to me that she was Jordanian."

On a trip home to Jordan after her junior year at Smith, Luma realized that she had changed so much she could never feel comfortable living there. Jordan, while a modern Middle Eastern state, was not an easy place for a woman used to Western freedoms. Opportunities for women were limited. Much of Jordan's civil code was based on Islamic law. Under sharia law, which applied to domestic and inheritance matters, the testimony of two women carried the weight of that of one man. A wife had to obtain permission from her husband to apply for a passport. And so-called honor killings were still viewed as minor crimes in Sharia courts.

To Luma, a future in Jordan felt limited, whereas the

United States seemed full of possibility. Before she left to return to Smith for her senior year, Luma spoke to her friends one by one and paid a visit to her grandmother. She didn't tell them she was saying goodbye.

In June 1997, a few weeks after graduating from Smith, Luma gave her parents the news by telephone: she was staying in the United States—not for a little while, but forever.

Hassan al-Mufleh was devastated.

"I felt as if the earth swallowed me," he said.

Hassan soon became angry. He believed he had given every opportunity to his daughter. He had sent her to the best schools and had encouraged her to go to college in the United States. He took her decision to stay in the States as a slap in the face. Luma tried to explain that she felt it was important to see if she could support herself. Hassan would have none of it. If Luma wanted to see how independent she could be, he told her, he was content to help her find out. He let her know that she would be cut off from family funds if she didn't return home. Luma refused to budge. She didn't feel that she could be herself in Amman, and she was willing to endure a split with her family to live in a place where she could lead the life she pleased. Hassan followed through on his word by cutting Luma off completely—no more money, no more phone calls. He was finished with his daughter.

For Luma, the change in lifestyle was abrupt. In an instant, she was on her own. "I went from being able to walk into any restaurant and store in the United States and buy whatever I wanted to having nothing," she said.

After graduation, Luma went to stay with her friend

Misty in Highlands, North Carolina, a small resort town in the Blue Ridge Mountains where Misty had found work. Luma didn't yet have a permit to work legally in the United States, so she found herself looking for the sorts of jobs available to illegal immigrants, settling on a position washing dishes and cleaning toilets at a local restaurant called the Mountaineer. Luma enjoyed the calm and quiet of the mountains but sometimes felt lonely.

After a summer in Highlands, Luma kicked around aimlessly, moving to Boston, then back to North Carolina.

In 1999, she decided to move to Atlanta for no other reason than that she liked the weather, which reminded her of Amman. When Luma told her friends of her plan, they were against it, worried that a Muslim woman from Jordan wouldn't fit in in the Deep South.

"I said, 'Are you crazy?'" Misty recalled.

Luma wasn't sure. She arrived in Atlanta without a plan. She found a tiny apartment near Decatur, a suburb east of Atlanta. She knew nothing yet about Clarkston, the town just down the road that had been transformed by refugees, people like herself. Luma was determined to make it on her own. Going home wasn't an option.

2

Beatrice and Her Boys

In 1997, around the same time Luma was graduating from Smith College in Massachusetts, a woman named Beatrice Ziaty was struggling with her husband and sons—Jeremiah, Mandela, Darlington, and Erich—to survive in the middle of a civil war in Monrovia, the capital of Liberia. Rival rebel armies had destroyed the city, and soldiers roamed the streets. Bullets often hit civilians, and mortars pierced family homes. One night, the Ziatys were startled by a knock at the door.

Beatrice's husband was a paymaster, a man whose job it was to hand out wages to employees of the former government, and the men at the door wanted whatever cash he could get. Yelling, waving machine guns, and wearing disguises, the men seemed like something out of a nightmare.

Beatrice couldn't make out whether they belonged to an army or were simply common thugs.

"You got all the government money—we got to get rid of you," one of the men said to Ziaty.

Liberia was founded in 1821 by a group of Americans as a colony for freed slaves, who lived there first under white American rule and then, after 1847, under their own authority but with American backing.

Americo-Liberian rule came to a brutal end on April 12, 1980, when Samuel Doe, an army sergeant who had been trained by American Green Berets, stormed the presidential compound in Monrovia with soldiers, brutally killed Liberian president William Tolbert, and proclaimed himself the country's new leader. Doe was a member of the Krahn tribe, a tiny ethnic group that composed just 4 percent of the population, far less than the larger tribes in Liberia, the Gio and the Mano.

Soon a former associate of Doe's named Charles Taylor began fighting against the new regime. Taylor, a Liberian, had gone to college in Massachusetts and New Hampshire and, after being convicted in an embezzling scheme, escaped an American jail through a window, using a hacksaw and a rope of knotted bedsheets.

Taylor launched his rebellion with just 150 soldiers in a Gio section of the country. The group's brutal motto was simply Kill the Krahn. Taylor's force grew quickly, in no small part augmented by boys whom he armed and drugged into a killing frenzy. Some of these boy soldiers were orphans whose parents had been killed by Doe; others were kidnapped from their families by Taylor's own militias. By 1990 Taylor had laid siege to Monrovia. The city's water supply was cut off. There was no food or medicine. Soldiers terrorized citizens and looted at will. More than one hundred thousand Krahn refugees flooded into neighboring Ivory Coast, even as Doe's Krahn soldiers committed atrocities of their own. More than one hundred and fifty thousand Liberians died.

In 1996, Taylor made another attack on Monrovia and the Krahn who lived there.

Monrovia became a wrecked city.

Beatrice Ziaty and her husband were Krahn and remained in the part of Monrovia under Krahn control. During the siege of 1996, they hid in their house as battles raged outside. When their youngest son, Jeremiah, fell sick, Beatrice could do nothing but pray. It was too dangerous to go outside for help.

"There was no food, no medicine, nothing," she said. "I saw my child sick for five days. When that child doesn't die, then you tell God, 'Thank you.'"

Eventually, though, even the Ziatys' home became dangerous. The men who came in the night for Beatrice's husband began to beat him when he said he didn't have access to government money. Beatrice panicked. She grabbed Jeremiah and Mandela, her next oldest child, and ran for the back door, which let out into an alley full of shadows. The last words she heard her husband speak echo in her mind today as clearly as when she heard them that night.

"Oh, what do you do!" he cried. "They are killing me! Oh—they are killing me!"

* * *

With Jeremiah and Mandela, Beatrice ran through the darkened streets of Monrovia, past checkpoints manned by menacing teenage boys and young men burdened by the weight of guns too big for their small frames. The soldiers were content to let the Krahn leave Monrovia. Beatrice and her sons made it out of town and began walking east, toward the border with Ivory Coast. They searched for food and hitched rides when they could. But mostly they walked through the bush. After ten days of travel, they arrived at an overflowing refugee camp across the border.

With the help of other refugees, Beatrice and her sons built a mud hut for shelter. Then they waited—for what, they weren't exactly sure. The end of the war—if it ever occurred—wouldn't be enough to lure them back to Monrovia. Beatrice's husband was gone. The city was destroyed. Charles Taylor would come to power in an election in 1997, winning largely because people feared he would restart a civil war if he lost. He used the power of his post to continue the killing until he fell out of favor with the United States. He went into exile in Nigeria, was indicted for war crimes by the United Nations, and was eventually captured in an SUV stashed with cash and heroin on the Nigeria-Cameroon border.

Beatrice passed the time in the camp by standing in lines to apply for resettlement by the UN. She knew the odds that she would be selected were small—but what else was there to do? The camp, home to more than twenty thousand refugees from the war in Liberia, was dirty, with food shortages and the quiet threat of soldiers who worked in the camp to recruit young men back into the war. Education for her boys was next to impossible. Beatrice focused on surviving, protecting her sons from recruitment, and getting out.

Beatrice and her sons spent five years in that camp. Against all odds and after countless interviews with UN personnel, she learned that she and her boys had been accepted for resettlement by the United Nations High Commissioner for Refugees. They would be sent first to Abidjan, the largest city in Ivory Coast; from there they would fly to New York and then to Atlanta, Georgia, en route to their new home in Clarkston, a place they had never heard of.

The Ziatys' resettlement followed a typical path. They were granted a $3,016 loan by the U.S. Office of Refugee Resettlement for four one-way plane tickets to the United States. (Beatrice repaid the money in three years.) The family was assigned to an International Rescue Committee caseworker who would help them resettle in the United States. On September 28, 2003, the Ziatys began the journey from Abidjan to Atlanta. Two days later, tired and confused, they met the IRC caseworker at the airport. The woman drove them past downtown Atlanta, with its huge skyscrapers and gleaming gold-domed capitol building, to their new home, a two-bedroom dwelling in Clarkston's Wyncrest Apartments. The cupboards had been stocked with canned goods. The walls were dingy and bare. There were some old sofas to sit on, and mattresses on the floor. The Ziatys stretched out on them and went to sleep.

Beatrice began her job search almost immediately. Like all refugees accepted into the United States for resettlement, she would have only three months of government financial assistance to help her get on her feet, to say nothing of the debt she owed on the plane tickets. With the IRC's help, she landed a job as a maid at the Ritz-Carlton hotel in the Buckhead section of Atlanta. It was an hour's commute by bus from Clarkston.

Beatrice wasn't worried about the work, but she didn't like the idea of leaving her boys behind. They were going to school during the day, but she wouldn't get home from work until well after dark. She told them to stay inside until she returned in the evening. Beatrice didn't know how to use the bus system in Atlanta, but a fellow Liberian offered to show her the way from Wyncrest to the bus stop on her first day of work. At five-thirty a.m. she set out for the Ritz.

The work there was hard. Maids were expected to clean fifteen to sixteen rooms a day by themselves, and though the shifts were supposed to be eight hours long, in reality it took much longer to clean so many rooms. Beatrice's back ached when she returned to the bus stop at around ten o'clock. Without her friend to guide her this time, she was on her own. As she rode the bus through the strange landscape of Atlanta, she tried to put the fear of the past few years out of her mind. She allowed herself to think that maybe she and her family were finally safe.

The bus heaved to a stop in Clarkston. Beatrice got off, hopeful that she had chosen the right stop. She looked around and tried to recall the way to her apartment, then set out haltingly along the sidewalk.

It was a cool October night filled with the sounds of chirping crickets and the whoosh of passing cars. Beatrice heard a noise and looked over her shoulder. A man was following her. She sped up and clutched her bag. It contained her new driver's license, social security card, work permit, and all the cash she had. She felt the man's hand on her arm.

"Halt," he said. "Give me the purse."

Beatrice let go of the bag and braced for a blow that never came. The man ran, and she took off running in the opposite direction. Eventually she stopped, out of breath, and began to sob between gasps for air. She didn't know where she was, or how to call the police. She was tired, and tired of running. A stranger, another man, found her and asked what had happened. He was friendly, and called the police. The officers took Beatrice home and offered to help find the mugger. But she hadn't gotten a good look at him. She only knew his accent was African.

The incident robbed Beatrice of the hope her family would be safe in her new home. She became obsessed with her boys' safety. In Liberia, a neighbor would always look after her kids if she needed to leave them to run an errand or visit a friend. But Beatrice didn't know anyone in Clarkston. Many of her new neighbors didn't speak English, and some of the ones who did frightened her. There was plenty of gang activity in and around Wyncrest. For all Beatrice knew, the man who mugged her lived in the next building over. She didn't trust the police either. She'd been told by Liberians she'd met that the police would take your children away if you left them alone. So she told the boys and told them again: when you come home from school, go into the apartment, lock the door, and stay inside.

3

"Small Town . . . Big Heart"

Before refugees like Beatrice Ziaty started arriving, Mayor Lee Swaney liked to say Clarkston, Georgia, was "just a sleepy little town by the railroad tracks."

Those tracks still carry a dozen or so freight trains a day, which rattle windows and stop traffic. While many small towns around Atlanta have been absorbed into the city or big county governments, Clarkston has retained its independence. Clarkston residents elect their own mayor and city council and have their own police department. A pastoral suburb of around 7,200 amid a city of some five million people, Clarkston is still its own town.

Clarkston was originally settled by yeoman farmers and railroad workers in the years after the Civil War. For much of the next century, little of importance happened in Clarkston.

It was a typical small southern town, conservative and white. Folks in Clarkston sent their kids to Clarkston High School, went to services at one of the churches on Church Street, and bought their groceries at a local independent grocery store called Thriftown. Life in Clarkston was simple, and few from the outside world paid the town much attention, which suited the residents of Clarkston just fine.

That began to change in the 1970s, when the Atlanta airport expanded to become the Southeast's first international hub and, eventually, one of the world's busiest airports. The airport brought jobs, and the people working those new jobs needed places to live. A few investors bought up tracts of cheap land in Clarkston because of the town's location, just outside a beltway that encircles the city and offers easy access to the airport and downtown. They built a series of apartment complexes—mostly two-story buildings arranged around big parking lots.

Middle-class whites moved in, and over time the population of Clarkston more than doubled. In the 1980s white people began to leave the apartments in Clarkston. Crime was rising, and newer suburbs farther from town were roomier and less diverse. Middle-class whites in Clarkston, flush from Atlanta's economic boom following the expansion of the airport, could afford to move. Vacancies rose and rents fell. Crime surged. Landlords filled the apartment complexes through government housing programs and cut back on upkeep, allowing the complexes to fall into disrepair. Pretty soon Clarkston, or at least the Clarkston apartment complexes, found itself caught in a cycle of urban decay. In the late 1980s, another group of outsiders took note of Clarkston:

the nonprofit agencies that resettle the tens of thousands of refugees accepted into the United States each year. The agencies—which include the International Rescue Committee, the organization founded in 1933 by Albert Einstein to help bring Jewish refugees from Europe to the United States; World Relief; Lutheran Family Services; and others—are contracted by the government to help refugee families settle into their new lives. They help find the families schools, jobs, and access to social services. But first they have to find a place for the families to live.

From the perspective of the resettlement agencies, Clarkston, Georgia, was a perfect community in which to place refugees who were just arriving in the United States. It was thirteen miles from downtown Atlanta, a city with a growing economy and a need for low-skilled workers. Atlanta had public transportation in the form of bus and rail, which made getting to those jobs easy, and Clarkston had its own rail stop—at the end of the line. With all those decaying apartment complexes in town, Clarkston had a surplus of cheap housing. And the town had enough navigable sidewalks to qualify as pedestrian-friendly—important for a large group of people who couldn't afford automobiles. The apartment complexes were within walking distance of the main shopping center, so residents could get their food without hitching a ride or taking a train or bus.

The first refugees arrived in Clarkston in the late 1980s and early 1990s from Southeast Asia—mostly Vietnamese and Cambodians fleeing Communist governments. Their resettlement went smoothly, and none of the older residents raised any objection, if they even noticed these newcomers.

After all, the apartments the refugees lived in were a world away from the houses across town. So the agencies, encouraged by the success of that early round of resettlement, brought in other refugees—survivors of the conflicts in Bosnia and Kosovo, and oppressed minorities from the former Soviet Union. World Relief and the International Rescue Committee opened offices in Clarkston to better serve the newcomers, and resettled still more refugees—from war-ravaged African countries including Liberia, Congo, Burundi, Sudan, Somalia, Ethiopia, and Eritrea. Between 1996 and 2001, more than nineteen thousand refugees were resettled in Georgia, and many of those ended up in or around Clarkston. The 2000 census revealed that one-third of Clarkston's population was foreign-born, though almost everyone suspected the number was higher because census estimates did not account for large numbers of refugees and immigrants living together. In a relatively short amount of time, Clarkston had completely changed.

While the freight trains continued to rumble through town a dozen times a day, little in Clarkston looked familiar to the people who'd spent their lives there. Women walked down the street in hijabs and even in full burkas, or *jalabib*. The shopping center transformed: while Thriftown, the grocery store, remained, restaurants such as Hungry Harry's pizza joint were replaced by Vietnamese and Eritrean restaurants, a halal butcher, and a "global pharmacy" that catered to the refugee community by selling, among other things, international phone cards. A mosque opened up on Indian Creek Drive, just across the street from the elementary and high schools, and began to draw hundreds of worshipers.

(Longtime Clarkston residents now know to avoid Indian Creek Drive on Friday afternoons because of the traffic jam caused by Friday prayers.) As newcomers arrived, many older white residents simply left, and the demographic change was reflected in nearly all of Clarkston's institutions. Clarkston High School became home to students from more than fifty countries. A third of the students at the local elementary school skip lunch during Ramadan. Attendance at the old Clarkston Baptist Church dwindled from around seven hundred to fewer than a hundred.

While many of the changes in Clarkston were hard to notice at first, certain events caused locals to wonder what exactly was happening to their town. A group of Bosnian refugees who had come from the town of Bosanski Samac came face to face in Clarkston with a Serbian soldier named Nikola Vukovic, who they said had tortured them during the war, beating them bloody in the town police station for days. (They eventually sued Vukovic, who was living just outside of Clarkston in the town of Stone Mountain and laboring at a compressor factory for eight dollars an hour. They won a $140 million judgment, but never collected; Vukovic fled the United States.)

The citizens of many communities might have organized, or protested, or somehow pushed back, but Clarkston wasn't a protesting kind of place. The town's quiet, conservative southern character didn't go in for rallies and bullhorns. Rather than making noise, during the first decade of resettlement the older residents of Clarkston simply retreated into their homes.

Councilwoman Karen Feltz remembers that when she

moved to Clarkston from the nearby Atlanta neighborhood of Five Points—a community with a vibrant nightlife, and one where neighbors say hello and look after each other—she was struck by the strange quiet of her neighbors. Few people talked. A sense of community was missing. It took a while, but Feltz said she came to realize that people were simply afraid.

"You're talking about people living their safe, quiet lives in their white-bread houses, and all of a sudden every other person on the street is black, or Asian, or something they don't even recognize, and 'Oh, my God, let's just shut down and stay in our houses!'" Feltz said of her town.

In Clarkston, resentment was building toward the forces and people that had caused the town to change in the first place: the resettlement agencies and the refugees. For a surprisingly long time—the better part of a decade—townsfolk kept their anger to themselves. But as resentment built, it began to show.

The first signs of trouble surfaced in interactions between the refugees and the Clarkston Police Department in the late 1990s. The police chief at the time was a man named Charlie—or Chollie, to people in Clarkston—Nelson. The refugees were a constant problem, in Nelson's eyes. They didn't understand English. Many were poor drivers. Writing traffic tickets to refugees became one of Clarkston's more reliable sources of revenue. Nelson argued that he was simply enforcing the law. It wasn't his fault, he said, if some refugees hadn't learned the rules of the road in the United States. But the refugees felt singled out.

"A lot of our community members felt harassed,

discriminated against," said Salahadin Wazir, the imam of the Clarkston mosque. Members of his congregation were often ticketed for parking improperly around the mosque at Friday prayers. "They were all just pulled over for anything." Eventually, some members of the refugee community became so fed up that they decided to act. For many, doing so meant taking a leap of faith. Most had come from war-ravaged regions where the police and other authority figures not only were untrustworthy but had the power to destroy lives. To stand up to the police in America was to take the nation's promise of justice for all at face value. In one incident, a Somali cabdriver, after getting pulled over by a Clarkston police officer for reasons he thought to be made up, reached out to other cabbies from the Somali community on his CB radio. They quickly drove to the site of the police stop. The officer feared a riot might occur and let the driver off with a warning.

In 2001, Lee Swaney—a longtime city council member who called himself a champion of "old Clarkston," that is, Clarkston before the refugees—ran for mayor.

The owner of a heating and air-conditioning business, he had a big walrus-y mustache and sleepy eyes that made him look older than his sixty-eight years. He drove a big white pickup truck of the sort you might expect to see on a ranch, wore cowboy boots and an American flag lapel pin, and spoke with a thick, low-country accent that betrayed his South Carolina upbringing. Swaney's platform reflected his old-school values: he promised the citizens of Clarkston that if elected, he'd work hard to lure a good old-fashioned American hamburger joint to open up within the city limits.

A year and a half after Swaney took office, something

happened that pushed the tensions in Clarkston over the edge: refugee agency officials announced that they planned to relocate some seven hundred Somali Bantu to Georgia, many of them to Clarkston.

The Somali Bantu presented an extraordinary challenge for resettlement officials. An assemblage of agricultural tribes from the area of East Africa now comprising Tanzania, Malawi, and Mozambique, the Somali Bantu had been persecuted for more than three hundred years. Most recently, when the Somali civil war began in 1991, the warring factions forced the Somali Bantu off their land in the fertile Juba River valley. Amid the lawlessness and horrors of rape, torture, and killing, the Somali Bantu fled to the empty and dangerous open spaces of northeast Kenya and into four main refugee camps established there by the United Nations. This history of persecution and wandering had left them, on the whole, poor, deeply traumatized, and out of touch with the modern world. They had little in the way of education. Many lived their lives with no running water or electricity.

It was clear that Somali Bantu slated for resettlement in the United States would need a great deal of help. They would need to learn English and how to fill out job applications, and they would have to get used to the expectations of the American workplace. They would also have to cope with the extreme trauma they had experienced.

Few in Clarkston knew anything about the history of the Somali Bantu when they learned, through media reports, that another wave of refugees was coming to their town. But some, like Councilwoman Feltz, began to do research. What she found alarmed her. She understood that the Bantu would need a great deal of help, but she didn't know who was going to provide it. She started to ask questions. Feltz wanted first to know where in Clarkston the agencies planned to house the newly arrived refugees. The agencies said they would scatter the Bantu around the various apartment complexes in town, wherever they could find space. This worried Feltz.

"These people are afraid of the police to begin with," she said. "If something happened, they would never come forward and say anything. Who are they going to tell? They think everybody's out to get them. The people they're living with—who raped their women, stole their children, and murdered their men? Do you think they're going to say anything? These people would be living lives of terror!"

To Feltz and many others in Clarkston, the housing plan showed everything that was wrong with the way refugee resettlement was being handled in their town. The federal government didn't provide the agencies with enough money to do the work required of them, and the agencies knew little about the backgrounds of the people they were resettling and weren't willing to admit that they were too overwhelmed to do the job.

Anger over the Bantu resettlement plan prompted Mayor Swaney to act. He reached out to the heads of the agencies to see if they might be willing to answer questions from locals at a town hall meeting. They agreed. The day before the meeting, Mayor Swaney struck a hopeful tone in an interview with the *Atlanta Journal-Constitution*.

"Maybe we can find a way for everybody to work together, live together, and play together," he said.

*   *   *

On the evening of March 31, 2003, about a hundred and twenty Clarkston residents filed into an auditorium at Georgia Perimeter College and began to write their questions on index cards. The first question was "What can we do to keep refugees from coming to Clarkston?"

The tone of the meeting only got worse.

Eventually, the patience of everyone in attendance wore down. Some people who supported the refugees began to attack the other residents as uncaring, even racist.

"Aren't you happy you saved a life?" one refugee supporter growled at Rita Thomas, a longtime resident who had spoken out against the resettlement process.

"I certainly am," Thomas snapped. "But I would have liked for it to have been my choice."

4

Alone Down South

Luma al-Mufleh knew nothing of Clarkston or the refugees there when she moved to the nearby town of Decatur, only a few miles west of Clarkston down Ponce de Leon Avenue. She found a job waiting tables. She made a few friends and, as if by reflex, began looking around for opportunities to coach soccer. As it happened, the Decatur-DeKalb YMCA, just down the road from the old courthouse and the home of one of the oldest youth soccer programs in the state, was looking for a coach for their fourteen-and-under girls' team. Luma applied and got the job.

Luma coached the only way she knew how—by following the example set for her by Coach Brown. She was more demanding than any of the girls or their parents expected—she made her players run for thirty-five minutes and do sets of sit-ups, push-ups, and leg lifts before each practice. And she'd make them run longer if they were late to practice.

Luma's approach did not sit well with all of her players' parents.

"Parents would get upset about certain things she did," said Kim Miller, a researcher at the Centers for Disease Control and Prevention in Atlanta, whose daughter, Maritza, played on Luma's team for three years. "They'd say, 'Oh, can you believe she made them run barefoot?' or 'Oh, can you believe she made them run laps because we were stuck in traffic?' Luma was really tough. They had to take responsibility for what they did. If you were angry with the coach, it wasn't 'Go home and tell your mom.' She didn't want to hear from the mommies. She wanted the girls to be responsible."

During Luma's first season as coach, her team lost every game. But over time, her methods began to pay off. Dedicated players returned, and those who didn't buy in to her system left. The players worked hard and improved. In her third season, Luma's team went undefeated and won their year-end tournament. "I don't usually use this word," said Kim Miller. "But it was magical. . . . She helped them thrive."

Now fifteen and an active soccer player, Maritza Miller describes her time on Luma's team as life changing. "She realized from the start that it's not something just on the field," Maritza said. "It's about trust. None of my other coaches thought that way."

Luma made the team the focus of her energies in those early days in Georgia. But soccer couldn't distract Luma from homesickness for her friends and family. Her parents still weren't speaking to her—they hung up on her when she called home—and she missed her younger sister Inam, who was now a teenager and no longer the little girl Luma remembered. Then, in 2002, Luma's grandmother Munawar, her lifeline to her family in Jordan, died.

When Luma was grieving, she liked to get into her daffodil-yellow Volkswagen Beetle, put on some music—something fast and peppy—and simply drive. She didn't know her way around Atlanta, but the strange mixture of gleaming glass office buildings, columned houses, stucco mansions, and long stretches of worn-out row houses gave her a sense of discovery.

On one of those trips, Luma found herself lost in what seemed to be a run-down area beyond the eastern side of the Perimeter, only a few miles east of Decatur. What she saw confused her. Women walked the streets in chadors and hijabs, while others wore colorful African robes and headdresses. Luma came upon a small Middle Eastern market called Talars. She pulled into the parking lot, went inside, and took a deep breath, filling her lungs with the old familiar smells of cardamom, turmeric, and cumin. Luma stocked up on groceries—pita bread, hummus, and *halloumi*, a salty sheep's and goat's milk cheese that was one of her favorites—then went home to make herself a meal like her grandmother might have made.

Luma became a regular customer at Talars, and each time she visited she again encountered the strange sight of African and Middle Eastern dress on the streets. But like most of the people who drove through Clarkston, Luma was too

preoccupied with her own worries to give much thought to
the unusual sights around her.

Luma decided to start her own business, a café that sold ice
cream and sandwiches, a place where people could spend the
day and relax without being hassled. She found an available
storefront in downtown Decatur midway between her apartment and the YMCA and cobbled together a group of investors from the friends and contacts she'd made around Atlanta,
including some of the parents of her players at the Y. In 2003
Luma opened her own café: Ashton's.

Running Ashton's was tough. Luma put in sixteen-hour
days, preparing food early in the morning and cleaning up
late after the close. She still wasn't speaking with her parents,
and her desire to prove her independence to her family in
Jordan drove her to work even harder. But the plan wasn't
working out. Ashton's wasn't pulling in enough customers to
make money, and Luma found herself working longer and
longer hours to keep the place afloat. She was still coaching
her girls' team in the evenings, and she was exhausted.

One afternoon Luma decided to drive to Talars to pick up
some of her favorite foods from back home. She drove past
the store, and had to make a U-turn in the parking lot of an
old apartment complex called the Lakes. While turning
around, she came across a group of boys playing soccer. The
boys were playing the game with the sweaty mixture of pas-
sion, joy, and friendship she recognized from the games
played in the empty lot on the other side of the fence from
her grandmother's house in Amman. But unlike in Amman,
the boys playing in Clarkston seemed to come from many

different backgrounds—they were white, black, and brown. Luma parked her car and watched.

"I stayed there for over an hour," she recalled. "They were barefoot, but they were having such a good time."

The sight of boys of so many ethnicities in one place began to open Luma's eyes to what was happening in Clarkston, just down the road from her own home.

"I'd never questioned why they had a Middle Eastern grocery store in Clarkston," she said. "I knew there were refugees, but I had no clue about the numbers."

On another trip to Talars, Luma pulled into the same parking lot. A game was under way. Luma reached into the backseat and retrieved a soccer ball, then got out of her car, approached the boys, and asked if she could join in. The boys were wary. She was a stranger—a grown-up and a woman to boot. There were crazy people in the apartment complexes in Clarkston—maybe she was one of those. But Luma also had a new ball, and the one the boys were playing with was scuffed and ragged. They allowed her to join in. Soon Luma was running herself sweaty, pleasantly lost in a game with strangers. "It reminded me what I missed about my community at home," she said. "And at the time I felt like such an outsider."

Over the next few weeks and months, Luma continued to stop in at the Lakes on her trips to Talars. She was getting to know the boys, learning bits about their pasts and their families' struggles. Gradually, they began to open up about their lives. Luma learned that the boys lived in all kinds of improvised family arrangements, often not with parents but with uncles, aunts, and cousins. She got a glimpse of the boys' desire to connect. The loneliness of being uprooted was something Luma understood. She also learned that pickup soccer in the town's parking lots was the only kind of soccer the refugee kids could afford; even the modest fees required to play soccer at the local public schools were too high for most of the boys' families.

Luma couldn't help but notice how much more passionate these boys were for the game compared with the girls she coached at the YMCA. They played whenever they could, as opposed to when they had to, and they didn't need a soccer complex or a formal practice to get inspired. Luma decided that the kids really needed a free soccer program of their own. She didn't know how to start or run such a program. She certainly couldn't fund it, and with a restaurant to run and a team of her own to coach, she hardly had time to spare. But the more she played soccer in the parking lots around Clarkston and the more she learned about the kids there, the more she felt a nagging urge to do something.

Eventually, Luma floated the idea of starting a small soccer program for the refugees to the mother of one of her players, who was on the board at the YMCA. To her surprise, the Y offered to commit enough money to rent the field at the community center in Clarkston and to buy equipment. Luma figured she could devote a few hours a week to a soccer program and still keep Ashton's running. She decided to give it a try. With the help of some friends, she crafted a flyer, in English, Vietnamese, Arabic, and French, announcing soccer tryouts at the Clarkston Community Center. She made copies and on a warm early-summer day drove around Clarkston in her Volkswagen and posted the flyers in the apartment complexes. She wasn't sure anyone would show up.

5

The Fugees Are Born

Perhaps no one in Clarkston was as excited to hear about the free soccer program as eight-year-old Jeremiah Ziaty. Jeremiah loved soccer. Since arriving in the United States with his mother, Beatrice, and older brothers, Mandela and Darlington, Jeremiah had been cooped up in his family's Clarkston apartment on strict orders from his mother. After she was mugged on her very first commute home from her job at the Ritz-Carlton hotel, Beatrice had taken a hard line. She wanted the boys inside when they got home from school. When Jeremiah asked his mother if he could try out for the new soccer team in town, she stood her ground.

"Certainly I say, Jeremiah," Beatrice told him, "you won't play soccer every day."

But soccer was one of the few things that could tempt Jeremiah into defying his mother.

*   *   *

Tryouts were to be held on the field of the Clarkston Community Center, an old brick and cream-colored clapboard building on Indian Creek Drive. At the time, the center was run by an energetic African American named Chris Holliday and governed by a board of trustees made up mostly of long-time Clarkston residents. But it was the refugee community that seemed to really embrace the center. Cooped up in small apartments around town, they were desperate for any place to go, eager to meet neighbors—or even better, real American locals—and they signed up for English and computer classes in large numbers.

When the community center offered a soccer program for young kids, "Refugee parents ran to get their kids enrolled," Holliday said, laughing at the memory. "I mean, we had moms *signing people up.*"

Along the way, though, some of the members of the board began to question Holliday's focus on programs for refugees. Art Hansen, a professor of migration studies at nearby Clark Atlanta University and a volunteer on the community center board in those days, said that he and other advocates for the refugees had begun to think of the community center as a kind of "refugee town hall." But at a dedication ceremony for the soccer field out back, Hansen said, he learned that not everyone in Clarkston felt the same way. When Hansen mentioned his delight at seeing a group of refugee children take the field to play soccer, he was rebuked by a couple of Clarkston residents who served on the center's board and the city council.

"They very clearly said they didn't like all these newcomers here," Hansen recalled. "There was this clear other sentiment saying, 'This is the old Clarkston High School. This is a Clarkston building. This belongs to the old Clarkston—the real Clarkston. Not to these newcomers.'"

But there was one reason that even the most suspicious community center supporters accepted the idea of a refugee soccer program on the new field: it was great public relations. The community center depended on foundation grants for funds, and refugee programs would help secure that money.

Luma pulled her Volkswagen Beetle into the center's parking lot on a sunny June afternoon in 2004, before her team's first tryouts. She wasn't sure what kind of response her flyers had generated among the boys in the complexes around Clarkston. They were naturally wary.

But on the other side of town, Jeremiah Ziaty had no doubt about his enthusiasm for the new team. His mother was still at work when he set out from the family's apartment, a small backpack on his shoulder, ready to play.

When Jeremiah arrived at the center, he joined twenty-two other boys on the small field behind the building. On the sideline, he unzipped his backpack carefully, as though it contained something fragile and precious, which in a way it did: a single black oversized sneaker. Jeremiah took off his flip-flops and slipped the shoe on his right foot, leaving his left foot bare, and took the field.

Before tryouts began, the boys seemed puzzled. Where, they wondered, was the coach? Luma was right in front of them, but a woman soccer coach was a strange sight to young Africans, and to young Muslim boys from Afghanistan and

Iraq. During a shooting drill, Luma was teaching the boys how to strike the ball with the tops of their feet when she overheard a Sudanese boy talking to the others.

"She's a girl," he said. "She doesn't know what she's talking about."

Luma ordered him to stand in goal. She took off her shoes as the boy waited beneath the crossbar, rocking back and forth and growing more anxious by the moment. She asked for a ball, which she placed on the grass. Then, barefoot, as the team looked on, she blasted a shot directly at the boy, who dove out of the way as the ball rocketed into the net. Luma turned toward her team. "Anybody else?" she asked.

On that first day of tryouts, Jeremiah played with all of the joyful abandon you might expect of an eight-year-old who had been stuck inside a dark two-bedroom apartment for months. Soon the other boys had given him a nickname— One Shoe—which Jeremiah didn't seem to mind in the least. Before heading home, he took his shoe off, carefully wiped it down, and placed it in his backpack before slipping on his flip-flops and starting the two-mile walk back home.

"See you later, Coach," he said to Luma as he left the field.

"See you later, One Shoe," she said.

Jeremiah made the team. But when Beatrice Ziaty found out her son was sneaking off to play soccer with strangers after school, she became angry. "You're too small," Beatrice scolded him. "Don't go out of the house!"

Jeremiah started to cry. He begged his mother to let him play, but Beatrice wasn't going to let anything bad happen to her son. And she certainly wasn't going to be defied—not after all she'd done to get the family here. Inside, though, Beatrice was torn. She knew an eight-year-old boy needed to run. She knew it wasn't fair to keep him confined to a small apartment all the time.

"You say you have a coach," she finally said to Jeremiah. "Why you can't bring the coach to me to see?"

"Momma," he said, "I will bring her."

The conversation between Beatrice and Luma took place outside, in front of the Ziatys' apartment. Luma came in her Beetle and parked out front. Beatrice walked outside with Jeremiah and explained her concerns to Coach Luma: she wanted to know that her son would be safe and with an adult. She wanted to know how to get in touch with Luma if something went wrong. And she wanted to make sure that Jeremiah wasn't walking alone through Clarkston.

"She did the bulk of the talking," Luma recalled. "She said that Jeremiah was her baby and she wanted to know where he was going."

Luma promised to pick Jeremiah up before practice and to drop him off afterward. He wouldn't have to walk alone. She gave Beatrice her cell phone number and promised to be reachable.

"I'll treat him like he's my own kid," Luma told her. "He's going to be my responsibility."

Beatrice agreed to the plan. Jeremiah climbed into Luma's Volkswagen and sat among the soccer balls and bright-orange plastic cones, and together they were off to practice. One Shoe had no intention of letting his mother down.

* * *

During those early practices, Luma made a point not to ask her players about their pasts. The soccer field, she felt, should be a place where they could leave all that behind. But as the kids became more comfortable with her, they would reveal details about their experiences that showed Luma how the trauma they'd experienced was still affecting them. Luma learned that Jeremiah had been at home the night that his father was killed. Once, at an early practice, Luma complained that a young Liberian player seemed to zone out during play. Another Liberian who knew the boy told her she didn't understand: the boy had been forced by soldiers to shoot a close friend. Luma wasn't a social worker, and she had no background in dealing with such intense trauma. At these moments, she felt in over her head.

"How do you react when someone tells you he saw his father get killed?" she said. "I didn't know."

Luma picked up on another problem facing her young players. Many had come from places that had been destroyed by war, so they had never had access to any kind of formal education. Often refugee children were unable to read or do even the simplest math. Without a basic education in their own language, they were playing catch-up in schools where classes were taught in a new language, one many of the boys could barely understand. While the public school system around Clarkston offered English-as-a-second-language programs, the schools were overwhelmed with newcomers. To move students through the system, many refugees were placed in standard classes that, while appropriate for their ages, did not take into account their lack of schooling or English. If these students didn't get help and find a way to succeed in school, they would fail out or simply get too old for high school, at which point they would be on their own.

Given the love for soccer in the refugee community, Luma wondered if the game and her team could attract some of these kids to after-school tutoring that might give them a better chance to succeed. She resolved to get help from volunteers and educators for tutoring before practices, and to require her players to attend or lose their spots on her team.

Somewhere along the way, the team got a name: the Fugees. Luma was unsure who exactly came up with the name, which many opposing teams assumed was a reference to the hip-hop band of the same name. But in fact it was simply short for "refugees."

That first season, the Fugees played in a recreational, or rec, league, an informal division teams played in before they could enter competition in the "select" grouping. There wasn't much of a budget, so Luma relied on donations, which didn't always work out. A batch of jerseys given to the Fugees turned out to be very large, almost like nightshirts. Someone donated a box of old cleats, but when one of the players went to kick a ball, the sole of his shoe flew into the air, making his teammates laugh; the shoes were so old that the glue holding them together had rotted.

Luma had to teach her team the basics of organized play—how to execute throw-ins, how to stay onside. But soon enough, a bigger challenge came up. Luma noticed that when she would tell the boys to divide into groups for drills, they would split up according to ethnic backgrounds or common languages. In scrimmages, boys would always pass to their own kind. And each group, she learned, had bad thoughts about the others.

"The Afghan and Iraqi kids would look down on the African kids," Luma said. "And kids from northern Africa would look down on kids from other parts of Africa. There was a lot of underlying racism and a lot of baggage they brought with them."

Somehow, Luma would have to find a way to get all these kids to play as a unit. "It was about trying to figure out what they have in common," she said.

While Luma was trying to find a way to get the kids to play together, she was also getting to know their parents, most of whom were single mothers. She quickly discovered that these women needed help—mostly in understanding paperwork. With her Arabic and French, Luma was able to translate documents and answer some of their questions. She made appointments with doctors and social workers. Luma gave her cell phone number to her players and their families, and soon they were calling with requests for help. Teachers learned to call Luma when her players' parents couldn't be found or were at work. The families showed their gratitude by offering Luma tea and inviting her to dinner. Luma felt needed, and couldn't help but notice how much better this kind of work felt than running Ashton's. In fact, Ashton's was losing money—and fast. Luma was worried. She didn't want to disappoint her investors, and she had wanted more than anything to prove to her parents that she could succeed on her own. But lately, she had begun to wonder how much longer she could keep the place open.

"I had never failed like that before," she said. "There was a lot of shame."

One afternoon Luma was driving Jeremiah home when he let slip that he was hungry. Luma told him he should eat when he got home, but Jeremiah said there wasn't any food there—that it was, in his words, "that time of the month." Luma asked what he meant, and Jeremiah explained that at a certain time each month, food stamps ran out. The family had to go hungry until another batch arrived. Luma was stunned. She had known that her players' families were poor, but she hadn't realized that they might actually be going hungry. She drove straight to the store and bought groceries for Jeremiah's family, but his words stayed with her. Each night at the café, she tossed away leftover food without a thought.

"You're worrying if you're going to have enough people coming in to buy three-dollar lattes when just down the road there are people who can't afford to eat," she said.

The conversation with Jeremiah settled Luma's mind on the question of Ashton's: it was time for her to admit her failure and walk away. But while the failure of Ashton's hurt Luma's ego, it was also an opportunity to focus her life on more important things. She wanted to start a business that could employ women like Beatrice, paying them fairly without making them commute halfway across Atlanta by bus or train. She had an idea for a simple cleaning business for homes and offices that would employ refugee mothers. She could find clients through her local contacts, and work side by side with her players' mothers, who could work in the daytime while their children were at school and get home to their families in the evenings.

But mostly, Luma wanted to coach the Fugees. She let her girls' team know she wouldn't be coaching them anymore. She was going to focus all of her energy on her new program.

"When I got to know the families and their struggles, I knew I couldn't fail," she said. "I couldn't quit when things didn't go right. I was on the hook to succeed."

6

"Coach Says It's Not Good"

On September 26, 2005, a tired twelve-year-old boy named Bienvenue Ntwari slowly opened the door of his Clarkston apartment and, squinting against the sun, took his first real look at America. Two days before, Bienvenue had set out with his mother, Generose, his older brother, Alex, and his younger brother, Ive (pronounced EE-vay), from a refugee camp in Mozambique.

The family landed in Atlanta at night. They were suddenly surrounded by unfamiliar sights, sounds, and languages. They walked through the long halls of the airport, past moving sidewalks, ads, stands of strange-looking food, and people who all seemed to know exactly where they wanted to go. The family was met by a caseworker from the International Rescue Committee, who helped them load their things into a

car and drove them through downtown Atlanta, toward
Clarkston. Along I-20, a superhighway that divides Atlanta
into north and south, cars whizzed past at frightening speeds.
The streets in America were so smooth. The family felt as
though they had been beamed into another world.

After a thirty-minute ride, the caseworker pulled into the
Willow Ridge apartment complex. The parking lot was quiet.
There was no one around. The family unloaded the car in a
daze and followed the caseworker through a doorway into a
stark ground-floor apartment with mattresses on the floor.
Generose, Alex, Bienvenue—"Bien" to friends and family—
and Ive fell onto the mattresses and slept.

The family was from Burundi, one of the poorest countries in the world. Burundi is about the size of Connecticut
and is home to some 8.5 million people. As in Rwanda, a
Tutsi minority ruled over a Hutu majority for decades. In
1993, Burundi held its first free elections, which produced
the country's first Hutu leader, Melchior Ndadaye.

Four months after he took office, Ndadaye was assassi-
nated by Tutsi radicals. Soon after his death was announced
by radio, enraged Hutus took their revenge by killing scores
of Tutsis. Tutsis then used their control of the military to
wipe out whole villages of Hutus. This tit-for-tat violence got
worse and worse. Within a year, one hundred thousand people had been killed. In the ensuing civil war, which lasted
until 2003, some three hundred thousand died, and countless
fled into the mountains or into refugee camps in Tanzania
and Mozambique.

In 2000, the killing was still going on. Hutu rebels fought
for control of the capital, Bujumbura, where Generose and

her family lived. Generose, whose fair skin and narrow facial features marked her as a Tutsi, fled the city with her boys.

The family made it to a refugee camp in Mozambique, where Generose applied for refugee status and—she hoped—resettlement in a safer country. Four years later, in August 2005, she learned that her application had been accepted. The family would be going to the United States, to a place called Atlanta. The journey took over a full day, as the family flew from South Africa to New York and then to Atlanta. It was the first time any of them had been on an airplane.

"All I remember," said Alex, now fifteen, "is that it was scary."

That first morning in their apartment outside Clarkston, Generose sleepily told her boys to get their things and get ready to leave again. The boys laughed. Generose hadn't understood that they had reached their final destination, that the empty apartment where they had spent the night and where they were now gathered was where they would live. They were home.

Bienvenue wondered how much of what he remembered from the night before had been real and how much a dream. He decided to look outside. He opened the front door of the apartment and was blinded by daylight. As his eyes adjusted, he saw a few cars. He saw some other buildings, and some trees in the distance. Bienvenue decided to go outside. He walked up the stairs to look around, and saw a boy about his age standing in the parking lot. Bien was very friendly. He decided to try a few words of English out on his new neighbor.

"Hello, what your name?" he asked.

"Grace," the boy said, saying it like the French, *Grahss*.
"Grace Balegamire."

"American?" Bien asked him.

"I'm from Congo," Grace said.

"Congo!" Bien said. *"Unasema Kiswahili?"* Do you speak
Swahili?

"Ndiyo," said Grace. Yes.

The boys stood and talked. Bien explained that he and his
family had just arrived the night before and that he didn't
know anyone or anything about America. He wanted to know
what American kids were like. Were they nice? Were they
different?

Grace laughed. Were they different! The boys at school,
he told Bien, wore their pants low around their hips—almost
to their knees, not like in Africa, where boys and men wore
their pants around their waists, with belts and tucked-in
shirts. American boys wore their hair long, in braids, like
women. They weren't so nice either. Some had guns. They
fought with one another. They made fun of people from Africa. Boys and girls got together and did things you weren't
supposed to do.

It wasn't at all what Bien had expected to hear.

"He told me here in America," Bien recalled later, "they
got some *bad action*."

Grace cut the conversation short. He was late, he said.

"For what?" Bien asked.

"Practice," Grace said.

"What practice?"

"Soccer practice," said Grace.

Bien loved soccer. In the camps in Mozambique, he'd

played the game barefoot with a ball made from plastic bags, in friendly but fierce matches between boys from Burundi and Congo. He wanted to know more. Grace explained: there was a soccer team for refugee kids like them, with lots of Africans and kids from places he'd never heard of. They played nearby. The coach was a woman. Grace offered to ask her if Bien could come to the next practice.

"I live over there," Bien said in Swahili, pointing toward the door beneath the stairwell behind them. "Come to my house and tell me what she says."

"Okay," Grace told him. "I will."

The boys went their separate ways, Grace to practice, and Bien to his new apartment to tell his brothers Alex and Ive about what he'd found. *There was a kid who spoke Swahili right outside, in the parking lot!* It was a big relief, and quickly transformed his view of what his life in America might be like.

"I thought we would be the only ones who spoke Swahili," Bien said. "We didn't think we'd have anybody to play with."

At practice that afternoon, Grace asked Luma if next time he could bring a kid from Willow Ridge who had just arrived from Burundi. He didn't speak English, but he liked soccer. Maybe he was good.

Luma heard about a lot of new kids. Caseworkers at the resettlement agencies often sent them to her, knowing that through the Fugees they might quickly make friends, that they'd be looked after, and that they'd get a chance to exercise and possibly some help dealing with the relocation. Luma's players frequently brought along new friends as well.

Bien had arrived in the middle of a season, when the Fugees' roster was full. But Luma agreed to let him practice with the Fugees even if he couldn't play in games. He would follow the same rules as everyone else and either show up on time or not come at all.

That evening after practice, Grace came home to Willow Ridge to find Bien and his older brother, Alex, in the parking lot. Grace told Bien the news. The next practice would be the day after tomorrow, he said. They could go together. Alex could join Luma's older team with Grace's big brother Josue. The team was pretty good, Grace said, and the coach was strict.

"The only thing I wanted was to play soccer," Bien said later, recalling that day. "I didn't ask too many questions."

The arrival of new players like Bien and his brother Alex brought fresh talent to Luma's soccer program, but also made things harder. Each newcomer changed the balance of the team, as players connected over shared languages or cultures. Luma developed rules on the fly to compensate. She didn't allow boys like Grace and Bien to speak to each other in Swahili; she made them speak English. She looked out for cliques, especially among players who wanted to stick with their own kind.

"I'd say, 'Get in groups of four for a passing drill,'" Luma said, "and every single time people would group up with people from their own country. So I started saying to myself, *I need a Liberian there, with a Congolese, an Afghan, and an Iraqi.*"

As the boys connected with Luma, they began to compete

for her approval. The boys on the Fugees—newly arrived refugees trying to find comfort and security in a strange place—really wanted Luma's blessing. She was in many ways a stand-in mother, and like brothers, the boys each wanted to be her favorite. When Luma spoke in Arabic to an Iraqi or a Sudanese player, boys who didn't understand felt left out. So Luma tried to make sure she didn't speak Arabic, even when it was easier, and she taught herself not to play favorites. For her teams to work, Luma realized, everyone would have to feel they were treated fairly.

Two of the most talented players on the oldest Fugees team—Jeremiah Ziaty's older brother Darlington and an Iraqi Kurd named Peshawa Hamad—spent months fighting with each other as they battled for Luma's approval.

"They were both incredibly athletic and incredibly talented," Luma said. "And they couldn't figure out which one I liked more. Darlington didn't like that Peshawa and I spoke the same language. Peshawa didn't like that I was close with Darlington's family. He would make comments about Darlington being dark-skinned. And they were both very selfish on the field."

As the team's biggest personalities, Peshawa and Darlington influenced other players, who felt they had to take sides. So Luma tried to get the two boys to work together. When she took groups of players out to movies, she made Peshawa and Darlington sit next to each other. When she was invited to Darlington's home for dinner, she brought Peshawa along. When Peshawa addressed her in Arabic, she responded in English. And in addition to these subtle gestures, she laid down the law.

"She said we're all foreigners, and this is a team where everybody unites," recalled Yousph Woldeyesus, an Ethiopian player. "And she told us she was going to kick us off the team if we didn't."

The next season, Darlington and Peshawa worked together to score, and their team went undefeated.

The challenges the Fugees faced—subpar gear, no cheering section, and the hostility they sometimes felt from opposing teams of American kids who resented the newcomers—only brought the boys closer. They sensed they had something to prove. Luma grew closer to her players' families too. Like them, Luma had left home for a new and sometimes strange place. She understood how it felt to be an outsider, and she valued friendships highly in this new place. Very poor families would prepare Luma dinners of rice, *mantu,* and freshly baked Afghan bread, of leafy African stews and *foofoo,* the porridge made from ground cassava root. And over time they learned what she liked. Beatrice Ziaty, for example, liked to make spicy stews, but she cut back on the peppers whenever Luma was coming over because she knew the coach couldn't handle the spicy food.

Luma's habits wore off on her young players in turn, in unexpected ways. Once, she took Jeremiah to the grocery store when she agreed to babysit him for a night for Beatrice. In the supermarket, Jeremiah asked his coach to buy bacon, one of his favorite foods, so they could have it for breakfast. Luma explained that as a Muslim, she didn't eat pork, and suggested they pick turkey bacon instead.

A few weeks later, Beatrice herself was at the store with

Jeremiah when she reached for a package of bacon at the meat counter.

"You can't eat that," Jeremiah told his mother. "Coach says it's not good."

Beatrice told her son that she liked pork—it was one of her favorite foods—and that as a Christian she was free to eat it as she pleased. But Jeremiah wouldn't budge: he told his mother he wouldn't be getting near the stuff; Coach said it was no good. The Ziatys had not had pork in their apartment since.

"Since Coach can't eat it, he will not eat it," Beatrice explained with a shrug. "So I don't buy it!"

7

Get Lost

In early 2006, problems began to develop between the Fugees and their hosts at the Clarkston Community Center, where the Fugees practiced. Emanuel Ransom, a board member who believed the refugee community didn't help enough with the center's upkeep, thought the Decatur-DeKalb YMCA, which sponsored the Fugees, should pay more for the program's use of the field. And after some refugee teenagers got into a fight near the field, Ransom insisted that the Y hire guards. The Y refused. While her sponsors and hosts argued, Luma tried to focus on her players and their families. But late in the spring season of 2006, she received a call from the YMCA telling her that the relationship between the Y and the center had broken down completely. The Fugees, Luma learned, were no longer welcome to play at the center at all.

Luma scurried to find a place for her team to practice. She eventually found an unused field a few miles outside of Clarkston and managed to borrow a bus from the YMCA to shuttle her players back and forth from the apartment complexes to practice. It wasn't a long-term solution; Luma didn't have unlimited use of a bus, and in the autumn season, a few months away, it would be dark by the time Luma could get the kids bused to the field. Luma didn't know what she would do then, so she focused on the remaining games and vowed to find a field over the summer.

After a short vacation at the end of the season, Luma had just a month to find the Fugees a new home field within walking distance of the apartment complexes where her players lived. Since the Fugees had almost no budget, Luma wouldn't be able to pay much, if anything, to rent a field. She had few options.

The YMCA offered to help out, and after a few weeks, they called Luma to let her know they'd found a solution: a field behind Indian Creek Elementary School, just across the Clarkston town line and on one of the town's main drags. Luma had driven past the school countless times without ever realizing there was a field behind it. One afternoon in July, she got in her car and drove to see her team's new home.

When she saw the field at Indian Creek Elementary, Luma was stunned. It was a rutted, gravelly field of gray Georgia chalk with a few tufts of grass and tall weeds. The field and surrounding asphalt track were covered with glass from broken bottles, and there were no soccer goals, only a couple of rusting chain-link backstops. Despite the conditions, the field was crowded. Members of the Clarkston refugee community were taking their afternoon strolls around the track. Young men were playing their own pickup games of soccer on the field. There was a jungle gym next to the track, where parents watched their toddlers play. A basketball court beside the field drew a crowd of young men who went back and forth between playing hoops and sitting in their cars. As one of few open spaces in Clarkston available to the public, the field at Indian Creek Elementary was certainly well used, but it was a rotten place for a youth soccer program.

Luma liked to run her practices in private, where her players wouldn't be distracted. But the field at Indian Creek was like the refugees' town square. Anyone could wander onto the field, and there was little Luma could do about it. The field did have a few things to recommend it. For one, it was easily accessible to the apartment complexes around Clarkston, some of which were visible through the pine trees on the field's northern side. The elementary school itself had classrooms where Luma could run tutoring for her kids before practice. Perhaps best of all, the field was free. The principal of Indian Creek had given the Fugees use of the field with the understanding that she wasn't offering much: there were no lights, no soccer goals, no bathrooms.

Luma resolved to put the best face on the new field. There were no bathroom time-outs during soccer games, she would tell her players, for example, so there would be no bathroom breaks during practice either. But if pressed, Luma would admit that having to use this field made her angry—at Mayor Swaney, at the folks who ran the community center, and even at her sponsors at the YMCA, who, she felt, should've worked harder to help keep the Fugees playing at the community center. Luma also felt that if a soccer team of well-to-do suburban kids was assigned to play on a field of sand and broken glass, their parents would call the team's sponsors or the league—*someone*—to protest. The parents of the Fugees' players were seen as powerless, she believed, so no one thought much about making the team play on such a bad field. Her team would be at a disadvantage.

The situation with the field showed something to Luma. She had hoped to build the Fugees into a well-organized program that provided refugee children with all the opportunities better-off American kids enjoyed. But for now, the Fugees' organization consisted of one woman. Luma realized she needed help. But she couldn't afford to pay a salary. She would have to find someone who cared about the work as much as she did.

In 2005, through the Balegamire family, Luma had met a Nebraskan named Tracy Ediger who had moved to Georgia to work with refugees. Tracy had grown up on a farm west of Lincoln in a religious family. She and her three sisters had attended church three times a week, rarely watched television, and had each enrolled at Christian colleges after high school. Tracy studied biochemistry and French, hoping to become a doctor. She soon realized that a career in medicine wasn't for her, but she didn't know what else to do with her life.

Tracy moved to Georgia to be with one of her sisters, who had decided to volunteer at Jubilee Partners, a Christian-run facility in the woods near Comer, Georgia, that worked with refugees. Tracy joined up as well and spent time teaching

English to just-arrived Somali Bantu refugees for fifteen dollars a week. The experience, she said, made her feel great.

"You'd sit on the porch, and you wouldn't be able to talk, but somehow you always felt welcome," she said. "In spite of what they've been through ... they were all generous and friendly and open. It's very different than the way people live in the U.S. because we're so driven and so busy all the time."

Tracy worked at Jubilee on that fifteen-dollar-a-week salary on and off for the next year and a half. She often went to Atlanta to check on refugees who had passed through Jubilee during their resettlement in Clarkston, people like Paula Balegamire from Congo, whose sons Grace and Josue now played for Luma on the Fugees. Through Paula, Tracy met Luma, who mentioned that she was looking for a coordinator for her soccer program, someone who could handle team logistics like travel and scheduling and be in charge of tutoring. Tracy wasn't sure—she was a country girl and didn't want to move to a big city like Atlanta—but she kept running into Luma through Paula's family. Each time, Luma mentioned that she was looking for help. As Luma and Tracy got to know each other, they found they had something powerful in common.

"We had the same feeling that with refugee families we felt at home in a way that we didn't feel in the rest of our lives," Tracy said. She was still on the fence in the spring of 2006 when she went to watch the Fugees play and to cheer Grace on. She liked the soccer, but there was a moment after the game that strongly affected her. The players were walking off the field at an old football stadium where youth soccer games were now played, when Tracy spotted Grace, whom she recalled as shy and scared.

"I was standing at the top of the stadium watching the kids walking up the steps and I saw the look on Grace's face and the way he was interacting with his teammates," Tracy said. "He was smiling this big smile and looked really happy. I thought, *I could do a tutoring program for these kids.*"

In the summer of 2006, Tracy agreed to join the Fugees for a year. She would have no salary—but she had no debts, and her car, a 1990 Chevrolet S-10 pickup she'd bought from her father for nine hundred dollars, was paid for. Tracy figured she could pick up a part-time job in Atlanta to make ends meet. For the Fugees, she would serve as team manager, a job that included everything from driving the YMCA's bus to running tutoring sessions for Luma's players.

"I didn't have any idea that this would take over my life," Tracy said.

In late July, Luma called a few of her established players to let them know about tryouts. Soon word spread to the parking lots and apartment complexes around town. Tryouts for the Fugees' fall season would take place the second week of August.

PART TWO

A New Season

8

"I Want to Be Part of the Fugees!"

For most of the Fugees, tryouts meant the end of weeks of boredom. There was little to do in Clarkston in the summers but sweat.

"We just stayed at home," Bien said, describing his summer. "We didn't do nothing. Without soccer, life was boring."

Bien could hardly wait for tryouts. There wasn't much drama in it for him—he knew that as a one-year veteran he would make the team. But he was curious to see what kind of new talent would show up, and to see the team's new field. Bien had grown up playing soccer in a refugee camp in Mozambique on a patch of bare earth with goals marked by small piles of rocks. He had been impressed with the field at the Clarkston Community Center. It had grass, proper soccer goals with nets, and lights overhead that allowed for practice when the sun set early in the fall. And he appreciated the grassy fields of the Fugees' competitors. By far his favorite, though, had been a field of artificial turf he'd played on at one away match. It was fast, and shots and passes rolled especially true on the smooth surface. When Bien got word that tryouts would be at the field behind Indian Creek Elementary, he stopped by to have a look.

Wow, he thought. *It's like Africa.*

As word of the upcoming Fugees tryouts spread around Clarkston, kids began to prepare. Some went jogging to get in shape. The pickup games in the parking lots around town began to attract more players and to get more intense. It wasn't just that the Fugees team was the only free soccer program in Clarkston. More than that, the Fugees offered a chance to play the game the way the pros did—on a grand scale, in a big open space with room for beautiful crosses, arcing corner kicks, and long, elegant shots that touched the tips of the keeper's fingers. The Fugees had practices and uniforms, and they traveled all over the state, a big draw to kids who rarely left Clarkston. The boys' parents understood that soccer with Luma was safe, unlike the games in the parking lots of the apartment complexes, which often took place near drug dealers and young men with too much time on their hands.

Luma would be coaching three different teams within the Fugees program—the Under Thirteen Fugees, for boys thirteen and younger; the Under Fifteens; and the Under Seventeens. There were veteran players returning to each squad—Bien, Grace, and Jeremiah on the Under Thirteens, for example; Alex Nicishatse, Bien's older brother, and Mandela Ziaty on the Under Fifteens, with team leaders Kanue Biah from Liberia and Natnael Mammo from Ethiopia. But Luma also needed to choose newcomers, few of whom had ever participated in organized soccer, and then find a way to get all of her players—rookies and veterans—to work together as a team. First and foremost, Luma needed players who would show up to practices and games on their own, since their parents were too busy to be of much help. The boys had to be willing to walk long distances if necessary, and to wake themselves up and get ready for games early on weekend mornings.

After the trauma of war and relocation, many refugee kids had severe problems. Luma had to keep this in mind. She had learned from experience that she needed about a third of her players to be well-adjusted kids from stable families. They would set an example for the others. Another third of the team would be boys who were for the most part dependable, even if they had a few problems at school or with other kids. The last third would be kids with real problems and unstable families. These were the boys who would require most of Luma's energy and who would most likely cause fighting on the teams. They were also the boys who needed the Fugees the most.

Luma's three teams had their own needs and goals. The Under Seventeens were the most mature, and would cause Luma the least amount of trouble. In previous seasons, most of the problem players had left or been kicked off the team. A few players on the Under Seventeens had cars. Luma expected this team to take care of itself. The Under Thirteen Fugees, Luma's youngest team, were a group of boys who had been with her from her first season two years before. Some, like Jeremiah, had been with Luma since her very first week of tryouts. Others, like Bienvenue, had joined along the way and made the team the center of their new lives in the United States. Their youth made them the most flexible and the most responsive to Luma's strict discipline. She knew their mothers well, since she frequently spoke to them when their sons acted out or broke the rules. The Under Thirteens had a star left forward in Josiah Saydee, another Liberian, whose awkward, toes-first gait masked amazing speed, as well as an experienced center midfielder in Qendrim Bushi, a stylish, mosquito-legged Kosovar who liked to wear bright-colored bandannas around his neck during practice. The Under Thirteens' weakness was on defense. The team's best defenders hadn't returned this season, so Luma had to find replacements from the pool of boys who turned up for tryouts.

The team was also weak at goalie—desperately so—but that was something Luma had chosen. Her goalies were Eldin Subasic, a Bosnian refugee and Qendrim's best friend, and Mafoday Jawneh, a heavyset refugee from Gambia with a bright smile and a sentimental streak—his older brother teased him for his habit of getting teary-eyed during episodes of *Oprah*. A goalie, even in youth soccer, needs to be aggressive and sometimes reckless, but Eldin and Mafoday were both gentle, happy souls. They could barely jump a foot. And yet, the two boys did everything Luma asked of them. They came to practice on time, didn't miss games, studied hard during the afternoon tutoring sessions Luma required her players to attend, and supported their teammates on and off the field. If the boys created a weak link in the Under Thirteens defense, the rest of the team would simply have to work harder on the field to support them. And if they did, Luma felt her team had a chance to win their division.

The Under Fifteens were a different story. They had an incredibly talented pool of players—if they decided to show up. Earlier in the summer, Luma had sent word around that she expected her players to get their hair cut short, a rule that hadn't gone over well with some of the Under Fifteens' best players. Prince, for example, a cat-quick Liberian and one of the team's best returning players, had spent the summer growing braids that crossed his head and dangled down the back of his neck in the style of Allen Iverson, the NBA point guard. The braids earned Prince some respect among his peers at school; girls liked them, and they hinted at gang affiliation, or at least comfort with a dangerous realm inhabited by many of his American peers. Prince had no intention of cutting his hair. He knew he was talented at soccer, and he fully expected Luma to make an exception and let him on the team. Furthermore, some of the other players—particularly fellow Liberians Mandela Ziaty and Fornatee Tarpeh—looked up to Prince. If he was kicked off the team, there was a chance they might quit.

"Some people want short hair, some people want braids," Fornatee said. "We don't all want to be the same. We want to be different. And playing soccer doesn't have anything to do with your hair."

Like teenagers everywhere, the Under Fifteens longed for

the respect of their peers and craved a sense of belonging, something that was especially hard for young refugees caught between the world of their parents and the new world of their friends and schoolmates. The boys on the Under Fifteens felt the conflict between the two worlds more strongly than their younger siblings, if only because they had spent more time in their home countries.

And finally, there was the lure of gangs. Luma had lost more than one of the teenage Fugees to gangs in the past; she knew she would be competing against the gangs again this season. If Luma could find a way to keep the Under Fifteens focused, and if she could find a way to create a sense of belonging and friendship that kept the boys away from gangs, the team could play incredible soccer.

It was a hot August afternoon in Atlanta when Luma stepped onto the field and looked over the group of boys who had turned up for tryouts. These kids arrived in blue jeans, long T-shirts, and baggy shorts that looked like pajama bottoms. One wore ankle-high brown hiking boots, as if he were about to go mountain climbing, while another stood ready to play in his socks, which flopped like clown shoes when he ran. Luma took down their names and ages, and with the help of the team manager, Tracy, wrote their names on strips of masking tape, which the women plastered across the backs of the boys' T-shirts. Luma had a few extra pairs of used soccer cleats; she waved over the young man in stocking feet and placed her foot next to his as a reference. In two years of coaching the Fugees, Luma had learned to eyeball a young man's shoe size with accuracy.

"You're a seven," she said to the boy before tossing him a pair of shoes.

Luma divided the boys into two groups and told them she wanted to see them play. As the boys took the field, she cleared her throat, squinted against the glare of the afternoon, and tried to ignore the negative thought that had been nagging her since tryouts began: *This is a rotten place to play soccer.* The "field" looked worse than it had the day Luma had first seen it. Summer thunderstorms had carved ruts into the baked earth, exposing bits of gravel and shelves of sandstone in the process. A salting of broken glass glinted in the summer sun. There was some grass around the field's perimeter, but most of the playing surface was dug out of dry Georgia chalk. White puffs were released beneath the boys' feet, until the field was covered by a cloud of dry dust that resembled fog. Every now and then, the dust coughed up a figure: a heavyset Iraqi man whose gray dishdasha dragged on the ground; a Sudanese man with a henna-dyed beard who walked laps on the track counterclockwise, a wooden staff in hand; and neighborhood kids who wandered freely through the scrimmage as though the field were any other right-of-way.

Luma blew her whistle and summoned the boys in. Sweating, panting, and covered in dust, they formed a circle around her at midfield.

"Prince," she said, addressing the Liberian veteran with a head of braids. "If your hair is not cut by the first day of practice, you're off the team."

The boys glanced at Prince, but no one said a word.

Practices would take place twice a week and would last three hours, Luma said. The first half of practice time would be for homework and tutoring. Luma had arranged volunteers for that. Tutoring was mandatory. The second half would be for soccer—and running, lots of running.

"If you miss a practice, you miss the next game," she told the boys. "If you miss two games, you're off the team.

"I have eleven spots," she added. "I'm not looking for a superstar. I'm looking for players who are willing to learn."

The final roster for the Fugees would be posted on the bulletin board of the Clarkston Public Library by ten a.m. on Friday, she told the boys—no reason to call before then.

"If you don't follow the rules, you're off the team," she said. "There are plenty of kids who want to play. If you do follow the rules, you're going to have a lot of fun."

Luma held up a stack of papers—contracts she expected her players to sign—and passed a sheet to each boy.

"If you can't live with this," she said, "I don't want you on this team."

Hands—white, brown, yellow, black—reached for the papers. As the boys read, their eyes widened.

I will have good behavior on and off the field.
I will not smoke.
I will not do drugs.
I will not drink alcohol.
I will not get anyone pregnant.
I will not use bad language.
My hair will be shorter than Coach's.

I will be on time.
I will listen to Coach.
I will try hard.
I will ask for help.
I want to be part of the Fugees!

9

Figure It Out
So You Can Fix It

"**W**hy you have to cut your hair?" Mandela Ziaty asked. "You play with your feet—the hair doesn't touch the ball."

"Who are you representing?" Kanue Biah said.

"I represent myself."

"No," said Kanue. "You represent your coach and your team."

Luma's hair rule had set off a debate among the veteran players on the Under Fifteen team. Prince had refused to cut his hair and wouldn't be joining the team. Without players from the previous season who'd moved away from Clarkston, the Under Fifteen team was suddenly very short on talent. The absence of Prince particularly upset Mandela and Fornatee Tarpeh. Neither Mandela nor Fornatee had long hair.

Mandela's mother, Beatrice, wouldn't allow him to grow his hair long; that wasn't acceptable for young men in Africa, and she didn't care what the American boys did. And Fornatee kept his hair cut so close to his scalp that he looked nearly bald. But the boys had counted on playing soccer with their friends and fellow Liberians, and now that Prince wasn't around, they blamed Luma and her rule that hair must be "shorter than Coach's."

Luma's hair *was* short—a couple of inches, maybe, trimmed above the ears and high on her neck. But she had her reasons for the rule. The Fugees had been the target of abuse from some of their opponents outside Atlanta for their accents and names; she didn't want to encourage hostility with hairstyles like the cornrows and braids that were worn by gang members in Clarkston and the rougher sections of Atlanta.

There was another reason Luma resolved to hold firm on the hair rule. The previous season, she had been so impressed by Prince's talent on the field that she allowed him to get away with skirting the team rules. He would leave tutoring early or skip it altogether, acts that undermined Luma's authority before the rest of the team. Players soon started to follow Prince's lead and challenge her. Luma counted the episode as a hard lesson, and vowed not to let any player, no matter how talented, get away with breaking team rules.

All Fornatee knew was that the hair rule was putting him in the uncomfortable position of having to choose between his coach and his friends. Fornatee had been in the United States for seven years, longer than most of his teammates, and was used to life in America. Few refugee kids in Clarkston knew anything about American football, but Fornatee had been around long enough to develop a strong allegiance to the Atlanta Falcons, the local NFL team. He'd even considered playing football for his high school that fall instead of rejoining the Fugees, but he'd re-upped for soccer, in part to play with Prince and in part because he knew he needed the Fugees, perhaps now more than ever.

Earlier in the summer, Fornatee's father had been in the backseat of a car driven by a friend when they were rear-ended by an out-of-control truck. He had been critically injured, suffering broken ribs and severe internal hemorrhaging, and had been in the hospital for a month. He was still weeks away from being sent home when tryouts came around. He faced a long recovery.

"I'm scared," Fornatee said. "My daddy can't work. I'm wondering where we gonna get the rent. They gonna put us out 'cause we can't pay the rent?"

Though he didn't like to admit it to his friends, Fornatee had come to depend on Luma. She was one of the few adults in Clarkston he trusted, a conclusion he'd come to after a simple gesture she'd made one day after practice. Fornatee had injured his hand when he fell during a scrimmage. He was used to just dealing with the pain when he hurt himself and letting whatever had been injured heal itself naturally. But after practice, Luma told him to get in her Beetle and drove him to a nearby pharmacy for first-aid supplies, an act of concern Fornatee had never forgotten.

"That's why I want to be on the team," he said. "She's more than a coach to me—she cares about you like she's your parent."

But Fornatee also felt loyalty to his fellow Liberians, Prince and Mandela, among others. It was a connection, he said, that was more powerful than the one he felt to his Fugees teammates from other countries. At times the Under Fifteens' differing backgrounds seemed unimportant compared to the things that bound them together. But the possibility that the team might break up into cliques based on country or tribe or language was always there.

"We're international and all that," Fornatee said of the Fugees. "But you hang out with people who speak your language and who come from your country. When we leave the field, I'm not going to call those other kids. They don't have my number, and I don't have theirs. That's just the way it is."

Prince was one of Fornatee's best friends. Both young men played offense. They'd planned to set each other up for goals and help each other on the field. And together they'd convinced other Liberian friends to try out for the team, only to have them bail out when they realized they'd have to get their hair cut. Fornatee wanted Prince and Coach to work things out. But he knew Prince wasn't going to cut his hair. It was up to Coach, he thought, to give in.

"I guarantee you," he said, "if Coach said, 'Don't cut your hair,' all those guys—Prince, everybody—they would come back."

The Fugees' preseason practices took place in miserable conditions. It was late August. The Georgia sun was hot, and still high enough in the sky in the late afternoon that its rays shone over the trees. Dust was everywhere. The players inhaled it as they played. It settled in their hair and eyes and on their clothes, giving sweat-soaked T-shirts the feel of wet, sandy beach towels. Mixed with sweat, the dust formed a paste that collected inside the boys' cleats, gnawing blisters into their ankles. And yet no one mentioned this quiet scourge—not Luma and not her players. It was as if all had made an agreement not to bring up the shortcomings of their new home.

The regimen for each of those early practices was the same. The Under Fifteens practiced on Tuesdays and Thursdays, the Thirteens and Seventeens on Mondays and Wednesdays. For the first half of the days on which Luma coached two teams, the Under Seventeens practiced first while the Thirteens received tutoring in an Indian Creek Elementary classroom from Tracy and whomever else she could find to volunteer to help the boys with their schoolwork. After an hour and a half, the younger boys came outside and ran their laps while the Under Seventeens scrimmaged under Luma's watchful eye. At the end of the scrimmage, the older players were dismissed to write in journals, which they did sitting on cross ties that surrounded the bark floor beneath the jungle gym. The Under Thirteens then finished their running and took the field for drills and instruction.

Practice for all the teams began with twenty-five minutes of running laps on the grass just inside the asphalt track. When boys misbehaved, Luma would run them to exhaustion.

The boys ran in silence, but they would jerk upright when they heard Luma call out a teammate's name for running too slowly. When the players had completed their laps, Luma ordered them to line up on the fringe of weeds at the field's edge. There she led them through sit-ups, push-ups, leg lifts, and bicycle kicks, walking up and down the line to push down the backs of players who tried to make their push-ups easier by bending up at the waist, or to stand over a player who was groaning during leg lifts, to make sure his heels never touched the ground.

After exercises, she laid out a line of small orange cones and ran the players through a series of drills: quick passes, headers, and chests. Practice ended with a scrimmage—the highlight of the afternoon for the boys. Luma divided the players into teams. The boys deposited two clumps of sweaty T-shirts in the dust at either end of the field to make the goals. Luma blew the whistle and let them play.

Play they did. Young men who had seemed exhausted after drills found enough energy to sprint up and down the field without pause. Boys who hadn't so much as grunted for the first two-thirds of practice now shouted for the ball. The commotion had a way of drawing in the rest of the neighborhood. Children on the jungle gym climbed higher to get a better view. Their parents and some of the older Clarkston refugees who'd come out for their evening exercise turned toward the field as well, or sat down on the cross ties parallel to the track to watch.

Luma expected her players to work hard and take practice seriously, and above all, to obey her. A player shouldn't have to speak perfect English to understand that goofing off in practice wasn't allowed, and if there was any doubt about that, Luma's sharp tone let all her players know when she meant business. When she sensed she was being tested, she responded swiftly, sending kids home or ordering them to run extra laps at the first sign of disobedience.

One afternoon as the Under Thirteen Fugees were running, Luma heard the boys cackling and shouting. A boy named Hussein, a small Meskhetian Turk with big eyes set wide apart, was skipping and thrashing his arms, making his teammates laugh.

"Hussein!" Luma barked. "Stop that—now!"

Hussein spoke only a few words of English, and it was unclear whether he understood Coach's order. Luma turned to the Under Seventeens, who were writing in their journals at the edge of the field. She heard a few muted laughs and turned back around to see Hussein still skipping and flapping his arms.

"Hussein!" Luma called again, raising her arm in the air and pointing in the direction of the apartment complexes north of the field. "Go home!"

Hussein came to a halt, and his expression turned to confusion as the other players ran past him, suddenly quiet. He dropped his head, then looked up, with pleading puppy-dog eyes.

"Go *home!*" Luma said, gesturing again with her arm. Hussein slouched over in defeat. He understood what his coach was saying. When he lifted his chin finally, Hussein looked like he might cry.

"Go *home,*" Luma said once more, her voice softening only slightly. Hussein turned, lowered his head, and began to walk toward the footpath that led to his apartment complex.

Luma was watching the Under Seventeens scrimmage at one early practice, when the Under Thirteens emerged from the school building to run laps after tutoring. The younger boys ran vigorously while they were in Luma's field of vision. But once they passed into the spot where she couldn't see them, they stopped running and began to walk. Just before they reached the area where she could see them again, they started running. Luma kept watching the scrimmage.

Soon Luma blew her whistle and dismissed the Under Seventeens from practice. Normally at this point she called the younger players in from their laps and started them on their drills. This time, though, she crossed her arms and wandered the field, looking at weeds, picking up rocks, kicking the sand—killing time. The younger team kept running: twenty-five minutes, thirty minutes, thirty-five . . . and so on. Eventually, the boys began to look at her, confused, in pain. Luma didn't respond, and they kept running . . . and running.

"Coach, what we did wrong?" Bienvenue finally yelled out from across the field as he held his cramping stomach.

Luma looked at her watch. Forty minutes of running.

"It took them this long to figure it out," she said, shaking her head in disbelief.

Luma blew her whistle and called in the Thirteens. From now on, she told them, they would no longer run laps around the track, out of view. Instead, they would run back and forth at one end of the field, in her direct line of sight, so she could keep an eye on them. The boys looked at one another with a mixture of guilt and anger, as if searching for the one among them who had suggested trying to put one over on their coach in the first place. It hadn't been such a bright idea after all.

"They need to figure it out so they can fix it," Luma said.

If Luma's way of teaching these lessons to her players seemed harsh, she made no apologies.

"These kids face so many hardships," she said. "Some of them are taking care of their siblings. They don't have Mom driving them in the SUV. So I'm not going to baby them, because they're never going to get babied. They need to grow up."

The Under Fifteens were also testing Luma. Even though he was no longer on the team, Prince hadn't exactly gone away. He had made a habit of stopping by practice and watching from a distance. He snickered as the Fugees groaned and sweated their way through laps and exercises. He showed up one day with a group of friends—guys and girls—who laughed and cut up in view of the practice field before wandering off to hang out as they pleased. Prince's teasing was a challenge to Fornatee and Mandela: were they going to cave in to the coach or hang out with their friends?

The challenge seemed to bother them both. Fornatee and Mandela began showing up late, talking back to Luma, grumbling and sulking through drills. During one practice, Mandela simply wandered off and joined in a pickup soccer game at the far end of the field. Fornatee invited some girls he liked to come watch him at practice; when Luma saw him chatting with them, she sent him home.

"My daddy don't care if I talk to girls," Fornatee said. "So why does she care?"

The other players were starting to notice Fornatee and Mandela's disrespect, and that was a bad omen heading into the team's season opener, just a week away. Luma had to decide what to do. Her first instinct was to blame the new field. The old field at the community center was fenced off and private. Prince wouldn't even have been allowed on the property. But she also felt a pang of sympathy for Prince. He was showing up, she suspected, because on some level he wanted to be on the Fugees, or at least to play soccer with his friends. There was a simple way he could do that, and it involved nothing more complicated than a pair of scissors. On that, Luma wouldn't budge.

Mandela Ziaty didn't like thinking of himself as a refugee. Refugees, to his mind, weren't American. They were poor. It was true that there had been times when Mandela's mother, Beatrice, was too broke to even buy food for her three sons. Mandela didn't want people to know about that, especially not his friends. Like a lot of fifteen-year-olds, he worried about what people thought of him. On school days, Mandela wore what American kids wore—long T-shirts that hung halfway to his knees, blue jeans so big and baggy that they slid off his hip bones, and clunky high-tops that he left untied so the laces trailed behind him. But when someone pulled out a camera at home, Mandela would go to his closet and pull out his church clothes—his clean white dress shirt with the crisp collar, his smooth black pleated slacks, and his shiny black shoes. He didn't want to look like a poor person. You never knew who might see a photograph.

Mandela didn't ask for help, and if he ever felt sorry for himself, he didn't let on. Instead, he got mad. When Mandela got mad, he got quiet.

"When he would get mad, oh, my God!" said Alex Nicishatse, Mandela's teammate. Alex laughed nervously at the thought. "Nobody would want to talk to him—they were afraid."

When Mandela's little brother, Jeremiah, joined the

Fugees, Mandela made fun of him. Soccer was wack, he said—for refugees. Jeremiah loved soccer and wanted his brother to play for the Fugees too, on the older boys' team. Mandela laughed at the idea.

"Mandela, from the beginning, he not wanted to play soccer," Beatrice recalled. "When Jeremiah come home, he would start mocking Jeremiah. Mandela say, 'As for me, I will play basketball.'"

Basketball was the popular game at school. Mandela had the frame for it too. He was tall, quick, and thickly built—the perfect power forward. But in the summer, there wasn't much basketball in Clarkston. Mandela was bored. Jeremiah kept at him. Beatrice had come to trust Luma, and she joined in.

"That lady—she's doing well," Beatrice told Mandela. "To keep you busy all the time is good!"

Restless, Mandela eventually gave in and joined the Under Fifteens. He didn't know the game well, but he had a natural ability. He could outrun most of the other kids. He used his big frame to ward off defenders the way a basketball player might block out for a rebound. His shot was powerful. Goalies learned to run from it. Luma had once caught a stray shot of Mandela's on the top of her thigh. She was bruised and sore for a week.

And yet Mandela never seemed fully comfortable. It was as though he wanted to be someplace else. When he was in one of his moods, he acted out in practice—talking back, showing little effort. Normally, Luma might have sent a kid like Mandela away. But she had grown close to Beatrice, and she hoped Mandela was just going through a phase. Mandela was one kid Luma was convinced she could help.

Mandela made friends on the Fugees—mostly with the other Liberian boys like Prince and Fornatee—and he made friends at school. But they weren't always the kind of friends Beatrice had hoped he would have. The boys hung out after practice, sometimes late into the night. Beatrice worried. She felt her son was hanging out with the wrong crowd. She didn't like the way the boys dressed—the ghetto look, with those low-hanging pants and untucked T-shirts—or their braids.

"I say, 'Is that a way we can dress in Africa?' No!" she said. "It's not a way that the men, they can dress. You can't hang your trousers right here." She pointed low on her hips. "We can't do that in Africa. Men always have the low haircuts. Men can't grow hair—it's for ladies!" If she were in Africa, Beatrice said, she would set Mandela straight.

"In Africa, when you tell your kid something and he doesn't want to listen, you will beat him—take the rod to him," she said. "Next time when you say 'Shhh,' he will not do it. But here, nothing, you cannot do that."

While their parents were at work, the kids were at school, learning the rules of the new culture, and sometimes using this new knowledge against their parents. Beatrice often felt she was at a disadvantage when dealing with Mandela. And so when he stayed out late or acted up, Beatrice called Luma for help.

"When I have problems with the children I will call her," Beatrice said. "I say, 'Please come to my aid. Mandela—he's going out too much, Luma.' And she says, 'I will.' So right now, she's really a sister to me. Because she take care of the children more than myself."

* * *

When Mandela acted out at practice, Luma appealed to Beatrice as well. The two women found themselves teaming up to try to keep Mandela out of trouble.

"Luma comes sometimes and says, 'I didn't like Mandela's way,'" Beatrice said. "Then I will apologize to her, and I will set Mandela down to make him understand the life we passed through."

The life we passed through. Mandela, Jeremiah, and Darlington heard that phrase all the time, especially when their mother was angry. Beatrice would sit them in a chair and tell them once again the story of the life they'd passed through. They knew it well by now, and exactly how she would tell it.

"We went from Monrovia, got to Ivory Coast, then stay in Ivory Coast for five years," Beatrice would preach to them. "You forgot. As for me, I didn't forgot.

"While you're sitting, you forgot all the bad things we passed through—you and myself!" she would say. "I think you forgot. But I not forgot. You forgot that we would go in the bush to look for food—you forgot. But I not forgot."

"Our country's here," Darlington, the oldest, would sometimes say. But Beatrice would go on: She'd remind them of the mud hut she'd built for them in the refugee camp, and how she used to break a single biscuit into four pieces, so they could all eat. She would remind them of what she had to go through to move to the United States—the countless interviews with UN officials asking her the same questions over and over again—and of all the worry she had that some small mistake would keep them in that refugee camp for years more. In Atlanta, she'd been working ten-hour days as a maid at the Ritz-Carlton Hotel all the way across town—one hour by bus, each way—cleaning sixteen rooms a shift. All for her family.

"You forgot," she told her boys. "But I not forgot."

Beatrice would go on until the boys became quiet, bowed their heads, and lowered their eyes. This simple gesture acknowledged her authority and the sacrifices she'd made.

"When you make a face like this"—Beatrice scrunched her brow, narrowed her eyes, and puckered her lips—"it means disrespect.

"When you bend your head down," she said, "you're *thinking*. You're *remembering*."

Beatrice wanted her boys to remember. Remembering meant respect for all she'd done, and respect, she hoped, would keep her boys out of trouble.

10

Meltdown

The field at Indian Creek Elementary couldn't be used for league games. So Luma arranged for the Fugees to host their home matches at Ebster Field, a perfectly maintained grass pitch in Decatur, a fifteen-minute drive from Clarkston toward downtown Atlanta. Luma got a YMCA bus to drive her players back and forth between Decatur and Clarkston, and gave them instructions to meet at the Clarkston Public Library at one p.m., an hour before game time. Anyone who was late, she told them, would be left behind.

The Under Fifteens' first regular-season game was on September 10, against the Gwinnett Phoenix, a club team from Lilburn, Georgia. Lilburn was only ten miles from Clarkston, but in many respects it was a world away. Lilburn was mostly white, middle- and upper-middle-class. It was also soccer country. The Gwinnett Soccer Association was founded in 2000, and was home to girls' and boys' teams of all ages that together had won more than a dozen state championships, as well as a 2001 national championship in girls' soccer.

A huge group of parents, siblings, and friends accompanied the Gwinnett Phoenix team to Decatur and set up camp on a sideline with folding chairs, blankets, coolers, and picnic lunches. The Fugees sideline, as usual, was empty.

Luma expected the YMCA bus to show up at Ebster Field by 1:15. At 1:30, though, the bus was still nowhere in sight. Luma looked at her watch and shook her head. The Phoenix took the field and began warming up. Luma pulled out her cell phone and called the bus driver to see what was going on. Some of the players hadn't shown up, he reported. He'd waited as long as he could and was now on his way, but without the whole team.

A few minutes later, the bus pulled up and the Under Fifteens began to climb off. Only nine players had shown up, two short of a full team. Mandela Ziaty had made the bus. He sat on the bleachers, counting players as he tied the laces of his cleats. Disgusted, he shook his head. Mandela had hoped that Fornatee and the others had gotten their own rides to the game. It was only now settling in that they simply hadn't shown up. Mandela was angry. Playing nine against eleven was not the way to win soccer games. Not only that— it was close to 95 degrees and very humid. With no substitutes, each member of the Fugees would have to play the whole game in the heat without a break. The Under Fifteens stood not just to lose, but to lose in a very tiring way.

Mandela sat next to me on the bleachers and asked to

borrow my cell phone. I let him, and he began frantically call-ing his teammates to see where they were. He reached Forna-tee at his apartment; Fornatee had missed the bus and was now stretched out on the sofa, watching television. Mandela asked me if I had a car. My rental car was parked within view. He wanted to know if I would drive him to pick up Fornatee and two other members of his team. If we left right away, he thought we could make it back by game time.

I hesitated, worried what Luma would think, whether my helping Mandela round up his teammates might look like I was helping them break the rules. Tracy, the Fugees' team manager, was nearby. I asked her advice; she said she thought it would be all right. Mandela and I jogged to the car and were off.

At 1:55, we pulled back alongside the field, with three new players, including Fornatee, in the backseat. The boys sprinted onto the field to join warm-ups, which were already in progress. Luma, though, wasn't with her players. Instead, she was standing in a corner of the field, giving no instruc-tions to the team.

"Coach," shouted Kanue Biah, the Liberian veteran, "why you not talking to us?"

"Because there's nothing to say," Luma replied. She turned her back on her players, walked to a set of bleachers in the shade at the far end of the field, and sat down.

Only Kanue seemed to understand that something seri-ous was going on. A veteran member of the Fugees, he was devoted to the team. Kanue was always on time, and more than any other player had bought into Luma's system. He decided to take charge.

A moment later, the referee called the players to the midfield stripe to go over their player cards. One by one, the boys stepped forward and said their names. The teams took their positions on the field, the referee blew the whistle, and the game was under way. Luma was still sitting far from the field in the shade, arms crossed, silent.

Minutes into the game, the Fugees were called for a foul in the box, setting up a penalty shot for the Phoenix. The Fugees' goalie dove left; the ball went right. The parents on the Phoenix sideline jumped to their feet and cheered. The Phoenix led 1–0.

The Fugees began playing more aggressively. They were called for one offside penalty, then another, and another. Fornatee shouted at the referee in protest and drew a yellow card, to cheers from the Phoenix sideline. A moment later, the Phoenix scored again: 2–0.

Mandela was angry now, and determined to get a shot on goal with or without help from his teammates. He took the ball on a pass from Fornatee and dashed up the middle of the field, fighting his way through the Phoenix defense and shielding the ball with his large frame. He dribbled to his right across the top of the box and blasted a shot high and to the right. Score: 2–1. The Phoenix responded minutes later, on a crisp cross to an unmarked forward right in front of the goal. The score was now 3–1. But just before the half, Fornatee got free up the middle. He made his move, quickly tapping the ball into an open space to his right: he had a wide-open shot. But he hesitated just enough to let the Phoenix goalie move out to cut off the angle.

"Shoot it!" his teammates yelled.

Fornatee took the shot, but it was blocked. The whistle blew twice, signaling the half.

The Fugees gathered near midfield and looked toward Luma. But Luma stayed where she was, head down, in the shade, refusing to even make eye contact with her players.

"You see our coach right there?" Fornatee fumed to his teammates. "She's got a job to do. I can't be the coach. You look at her—she's sitting right there!"

"Play on," Kanue said. "You've got to play on. You've got to come together."

"When you get the ball, kick it!" someone snapped at Fornatee.

"Coach has never did this to us," Fornatee said. "She's got a job. That's why she's a coach. This is her job!"

He paused and took a breath. The other Fugees stood in silence. "We're not going to worry about that," Fornatee said, collecting himself. "We're just going to play. Three to one isn't that much. I'm sorry, I had a shot. That won't happen again. If I'm open like that, I'm going to score, I promise y'all."

Everyone started shouting at once.

"One at a time!" Fornatee said, before taking the floor again himself. "Let me tell you something: Coach is just a coach. She cannot show us how to play soccer. Is she playing? No—we are. The skills we got, we don't need her. She's just going to talk. She cannot come on the field and play for us. We gotta play for ourselves. It don't make no difference if she's sitting down, because *she's not playing for us*! Don't no coach play. They coach, but they don't come in the game and play. We gotta do that for ourselves.

"She's trying to make us think that we can't play without her," he continued. "She's trying to test us, man. She's trying to make us realize that we need to win this.

"When the second half comes—we start scoring," Fornatee said. "We can win this, man. There's gotta be a reason why she's not coaching now. But it don't matter, man. We gotta win this game, man. We gotta *win this game*."

"Get your hands in here!" Kanue yelled. The young men formed a circle and stacked their hands one on top of the other.

"One, two, three," they chanted. "Go Fugees!"

Minutes into the second half, the Phoenix forwards picked their way through the Fugees' defense and tapped the ball into the left side of the net for an easy goal. The score was now 4–1. The Fugees were yelling at one another. After another offside call, Fornatee cursed at the referee, drawing his second yellow card and an ejection. The Phoenix parents and friends were quiet now; there was no need to pile on. The Fugees were tired, and without their coach, they were lost. The Phoenix scored again, and kept scoring. When the referee blew his whistle three times to signal the end of the game, the score was 7–2, Phoenix.

After the game, the Fugees gathered on their bench in silence, drinking water from plastic cups until Luma called to them from across the field to get on the bus. As the players filed off the field, I asked her what was going on.

"They show up to tutoring late," she said. "They're disrespectful. They show up to practice not dressed to play, their pants hanging down. I tell them practice is at five-thirty, they show up at six-thirty. I tell them, 'You have to be at the field at one o'clock for a two o'clock game,' and they're coming, what, like ten minutes before the game?

"It's not going to work," she said. "So I was like, 'You know, the way they're behaving is the way I'm going to behave. They're being irresponsible, and I'm not going to be accountable for them.'" She told me that she'd thought about going to get a hamburger, but the referee told her before the game that if she left the field her team would have to forfeit. So she decided to sit and watch what she knew would be a meltdown, especially on the part of Fornatee.

"He can't handle it when I get mad at him," she said. "They don't have the discipline to hack it. They don't show up to practices. They don't show up to the game. You can't compete like this."

With that, Luma walked away, trailing behind her players as they walked toward the bus. She waited for them to board and take their seats. A moment later, she climbed onto the bus to address her players and to give them the news. Luma had decided to cancel the Under Fifteens' season. They would forfeit the rest of their games. There would be no more practice or tutoring sessions. The Under Fifteens were finished.

11

"How Am I Going to Start All Over?"

Luma's decision to cancel the Under Fifteens' season was hard on many of the players, but it was especially tough on fifteen-year-old Kanue Biah.

Kanue was from Nimba County, in eastern Liberia. His family fled the war there when he was just two years old, for refugee camps first in Ivory Coast and eventually in Guinea. For reasons he rarely revealed, he was separated at some point from his parents and taken in by his uncle, a stern and demanding man named Barlea, and a great-aunt, whom he simply called Grandma. In 2004, Barlea was accepted for resettlement in the United States and placed in Clarkston. The plan was that he would eventually bring as many members of his extended family as possible to the United States. A year later, Kanue was accepted for resettlement as well, and joined

Barlea in a two-bedroom apartment in Clarkston. Asylum for those family members left behind did not come easily, or at all. Months passed, and none were granted entry into the States. So Barlea and Kanue, uncle and nephew, did the best they could on their own.

To support the two of them, and to have money left over to send back home, Barlea had an almost impossible work schedule. He took two jobs in back-to-back shifts at the Atlanta airport, an hour's commute by rail. He left the apartment each evening at seven p.m. and worked a shift cooking burgers at a fast-food restaurant. When that shift was over, Barlea then worked his second shift, in the morning, as a porter. He returned home each day around three p.m. and collapsed into bed for a few hours of sleep before waking up for another double shift. He was always tired, and a little cranky, particularly when dinner wasn't ready.

Kanue's role was to cook and keep the apartment. After classes each day at Avondale Middle, a public school, he went home and got to work making African food from recipes he'd learned from Grandma: beans and spicy stews of spinach and cassava leaves, which he poured over rice, and his favorite, peanut butter soup. He stored the meals in the refrigerator so they were ready for Barlea when he came in the door from his long night and morning of work. Barlea would heat the meals in a microwave and quickly eat—often too tired to say more than a few words to Kanue—before dashing off for his few hours of sleep. Kanue had kept up this routine from age thirteen. He was not allowed to play soccer, do homework, or leave the apartment until the cooking was done. Kanue never complained. In fact, his duties at home gave him a sense of responsibility and self-reliance that made him seem older than he was.

These qualities came in handy in the halls and classrooms of Avondale High School. Kanue was fortunate that as a Liberian, he was fluent in English. But his thick accent set him apart from American students, who teased him. Once, while reciting his lines in a school play, Kanue was mocked by another student because of his accent. He lashed out. There was a tussle, and Kanue was briefly suspended. But it wasn't in Kanue's nature to seethe or hold grudges. Instead, he tried something different, talking to kids who made fun of him so that he could learn from his mistakes.

"They say, 'You don't know how to speak English,'" Kanue said. "So I always say, 'When I speak wrong English, don't laugh at me—just correct me.'"

Not long after Kanue arrived in the United States, he was playing soccer in the parking lot of Southern Pines when one of the other kids told him he should come practice with the Fugees. It was summer, and tryouts were two months away, but the coach, Kanue learned, would let kids join summer practice so long as they understood that they weren't guaranteed a spot on the roster. They'd still have to prove themselves at tryouts. Kanue was determined to make the team. He began running to and from practice each day to get in better shape. At practice, Luma would ride her bicycle around the track for half an hour, setting the pace for her players, who ran behind her. In his mind, Kanue imagined himself overtaking her, and he tried his best each day to catch up with Luma. He was able to run farther and faster each week.

The Fugees offered a welcome opportunity to get out of

the apartment. Kanue made friends. He honed his cooking routine to free up time for soccer practice. And he was determined to stick around, even if a slot didn't open up on the roster.

"I said to Coach, 'If I don't make the team can I just practice with you?'" he recalled.

An opening did arise, eventually, as goalkeeper. It wasn't the best position for someone as physically fit and eager to play in the game as Kanue, but he happily accepted. He gave the position his all and became known among his teammates for toughness bordering on recklessness in his efforts to keep the ball out of the net. In his entire first season as keeper, Kanue gave up only three goals.

Once, the Fugees showed up to a game three players short a full roster. Luma decided to make adjustments and play eight against eleven. Thinking that she needed her best athletes up front if she hoped to stay in the game, Luma moved Kanue from keeper to striker. Kanue knew it was his chance. As a keeper, he had watched and learned the tricks and moves of successful offensive players, and had noted how the best had worked to keep a goalie off balance. He was determined to put that experience to work. In that first game as striker, Kanue managed to score his first goal. He was so elated that his celebratory dance drew a yellow card. The Fugees went on to win that game 4–2, despite being down three players. In the process Luma had discovered a new offensive weapon.

Over the course of his two years with the team, Kanue became completely devoted to the Fugees and to Luma. He showed up early for practices and was always on time to the bus for games. He rode his bike from his apartment complex near Clarkston to Decatur to watch the younger Fugees team play, and to help Coach carry gear. If the Fugees held a team car wash to raise money, Kanue washed more cars—and did it better—than any of the others. In games, he would chase the ball from one end of the field to the other, switching from defense to midfield to offense and back, running himself to exhaustion. Luma's biggest challenge with Kanue was keeping him from doing too much. She learned that his teammates would sometimes slack off, knowing that Kanue would step in to make up for their lack of effort. She had even benched Kanue midgame simply so her other players didn't start to rely on him. And she helped him too with Barlea. Once when Barlea told Kanue he couldn't play soccer because he hadn't made dinner yet, Luma stopped by with a roasted chicken for Barlea so Kanue could leave the apartment.

With no siblings in the United States, and a guardian who was hardly ever home, Kanue began to view the team as his family. "The Fugees—it's really important to me," he said. "When I play on that team, I'm with my brothers."

Luma's decision to cancel his team's season hit Kanue hard. She offered to let him join the Under Seventeens, but for Kanue it wasn't the same. Those boys were older and bigger than he was, and anyway, he wanted to play with the boys he'd become close to over the past two years.

"I was feeling really bad," Kanue said. "I was thinking, *How am I going to start all over?*"

The Sunday after Luma canceled the Under Fifteens' season was rainy. The apartment complexes of Clarkston were dreary. Kanue was at home by himself, bored, and upset about the demise of his team. The phone rang. It was Luma.

Luma asked Kanue if he wanted to see a movie; she was

picking up Mandela and Natnael, another team leader and a close friend of Kanue's. Kanue said sure, and he went outside on the balcony to wait for the sight of Luma's yellow Volkswagen.

The ride to the theater was quiet. No one mentioned the team. The movie was *Invincible,* a true story about a South Philadelphia bartender who went on to play for the Philadelphia Eagles. Luma didn't care much for American football, but she thought the boys might enjoy the plot. In truth, their minds were elsewhere. They were thinking about the Fugees.

It wasn't until they got back into Coach's car after the movie that Kanue finally asked Luma not to cancel the season. Luma told the three boys that she couldn't coach a team of players who wouldn't show up on time for practice or games. If she cut the bad apples from the team, there wouldn't be enough players for a full roster, she explained. And it wasn't fair to ask the remaining players to play an entire season with a short roster and no substitutes. Without a full roster, she told them, the Fugees would probably lose every game.

Kanue was ready with his own arguments.

"Canceling the whole team wouldn't be fair to us," he said. There were good kids on the team who followed her rules, he said. They shouldn't be punished because of the others. Kanue understood Coach's argument about playing with a short roster, but he had a solution. He, Mandela, and Natnael could round up a new roster of players. They could knock on doors in Clarkston and find good kids—kids who would follow Luma's rules. They could start all over again, with another day of tryouts. They would go back to the old players and tell them that if they weren't willing to obey the rules, they shouldn't show up. Kanue told Luma that he would read the contract to new recruits himself. If he had any doubts that they would abide by her rules, he wouldn't let them try out. Luma argued that it would take the boys ten days to get players and hold tryouts, by which time they would have had to forfeit two games—their season would be shot. And even then, how would a bunch of kids who had never played together compete with teams from Atlanta's best soccer academies—teams that had been playing together for years?

As the boys and Luma debated, Kanue took Luma's cell phone and quietly began to scroll through her contacts list, writing down the phone numbers of his teammates and other kids whose names he recognized.

Luma was torn. Canceling the team would send a clear message about her expectations to players on all of her teams, and she didn't want to appear to cave in. She was also worried about Kanue, Natnael, and Mandela recruiting new players, knowing that a team that had never played together could never compete with the well-coached and well-prepared teams in their division. Her players might get frustrated and lash out during a game.

On the other hand, Luma thought about the good kids, the ones who had done all she'd asked, like Kanue. She thought of Mandela, for whom the Fugees were a lifeline. She shuddered to think of what kind of trouble kids like Mandela might get into without the Fugees to keep them busy.

Luma decided to wait it out. There was a possibility that Kanue, Mandela, and Natnael might not round up enough new recruits. She told the boys that if they convinced the committed players on the team to return and rounded up new players who would follow her rules, she would be willing to hold another day of tryouts. She'd make her final decision about the team's season based on how those tryouts went. There were no guarantees, she said.

The boys were quiet for the rest of the ride home. Luma dropped them off one by one. When they got to Southern Pines, Kanue said goodbye, climbed out of the car, and dashed through the rain to the front door of Building D, where he lived. Barlea was at work, so Kanue had the apartment all to himself. He picked up the phone and began to work his way through the numbers he'd taken from Luma's phone.

"Bring all friends who want to join the team," he told everyone he called. "We're going to have tryouts. Coach is giving us another chance."

The Fifteens' season was on hold, but Luma still had two other teams to coach, and on Monday afternoon she stood on the field at Indian Creek Elementary as the younger of those, the Thirteens, completed their running. Luma summoned the players in with a blast of her whistle. The boys were joking with one another as they approached, but when they got close enough to read Luma's expression, they sensed that her mood was gloomy, and fell quiet.

"You're supposed to all line up and start running nonstop for twenty-five minutes—no walking," she said by way of greeting. "See how many of you are here? I don't have to take you all to the game on Saturday. I only have to take eleven. So if you decide to cuss, Jeremiah"—her bionic hearing had apparently picked up on some foul language from across the field—"you will be sent home.

"I don't know if you all know, but we no longer have an Under Fifteen team, and the reason is because of their behavior. So if you want to follow in their footsteps, go ahead—I don't have a problem with that. But then you too will no longer have a team. If you want to come out here and have fun, then play hard. If you want to take walks around the track, then go home. You're only practicing twice a week, so twice a week you run the whole time. No jogging. Real quick—if any of you lag you're going to take five more laps."

The Thirteens' first two games had not gone well. They tied their first game 4–4, and then gave up a one-goal lead in their second, to lose 3–1. The team wasn't passing well. Players weren't holding their positions, and they weren't talking to each other on the field. They had a long way to go. But the Thirteens seemed to get the message from Luma. It was time to get serious. Their Monday practice was quiet and intense. Two days later, on Wednesday, the boys showed up on time, ran hard, and were focused during their drills. The Thirteens seemed determined to let their coach know they weren't like the Fifteens. They were willing to do what she said, and they wanted to win.

The Thirteens' third game of the season took place on a hot Saturday afternoon at Ebster Field, the Fugees' home ground in downtown Decatur. The opponent was the Triumph, a mostly white team from nearby Tucker, Georgia. Luma gave her players their positions—Josiah, the tall Liberian with deceptive speed, at left forward; Jeremiah Ziaty on the right. Qendrim, the small Kosovar, would play center midfielder; Bienvenue, the happy-go-lucky Burundian, would direct the defense from the middle in back. The Thirteens' full roster had turned out for the game, so Luma was able to substitute freely, to keep her players fresh in the heat. To his surprise, even Santino, a quiet ten-year-old Sudanese boy who had arrived in the United States only a few weeks before the season, found his way into the rotation.

Only minutes into the game, Jeremiah took a throw-in on the far side, near the corner. He threw the ball to Josiah, who caught it neatly beneath his cleats and passed it back to Jeremiah, who fired a long, arcing shot that flew across the face of the goal and just inside the opposite pole: the Fugees were up 1–0. Before the half, tiny Qendrim dribbled through the defense ten yards out and tapped a slow roller past the goalie's left foot. The Fugees were up 2–0. Luma, though, wasn't satisfied.

"We've got one big problem going on," she told her team at halftime. "You guys are starting to play like them. You're starting to kick the ball wherever it goes. You're starting to walk around. You're starting to get lazy."

"You guys ready?" Luma asked her team finally.

"Yes!" they shouted in unison.

In the second half, the Fugees put on a show. Josiah slipped around his defender on the left side, and dribbled downfield at a full gallop before taking a clean shot into the right side of the net: 3–0, Fugees. Luma moved Bien up the field, from defense to offense, and he quickly made an amazing bicycle kick over his head. The ball flew straight to the goalie, but the move was so remarkable that the parents of the Triumph players applauded in appreciation. Jeremiah scored again, and late in the second half, Bien lobbed a cross across the face of the goal. Qendrim dove headfirst, arms at his sides, like a spear, and executed a perfect header—another score. When the whistle blew three times to signal the end of the game, the Under Thirteens had won, 5–1.

"Guys, you had a good game," Luma told them afterward. "It wasn't your best game, but it was a good game.

"We're going to keep working on our crosses, because we're getting there," she added. "Not bad. Next week will be a much better game—okay?"

12

Alex, Bien, and Ive

The apartment where Bienvenue lived with his brothers, Alex and Ive, his infant sister, Alyah, and his mother, Generose, looked almost exactly like it did the night they arrived from Burundi, a year and a half before. The walls were still bare but for a photograph of Bien that he himself had hung with tape in the living room, as well as a drawing in black crayon on a wall leading into the kitchen—a mural young Ive had started and abandoned but that had not yet been washed away. There was a TV on a stand in the corner, with rabbit-ears antennae on top and a VCR underneath, and three old sofas around the living room—all items that had been donated to the family by a local church.

Visiting Generose's family meant having a large meal cooked for you: rice or foofoo heaped with cassava leaves, potatoes soaked in tomato broth, beans, stewed greens with sardines, and often fried whole fish or beef in a sauce of onions, tomatoes, and garlic—though the family rarely had whole fish or beef on their own. Fresh meat was expensive and had to be saved for special occasions.

The first time I visited Bien and Alex at home, I was invited to sit down on a tattered sofa in the living room. Instead of landing on a soft cushion, I hit a piece of wood that hid beneath the fabric. When the boys saw me wince, they laughed. The sofa frame, a family joke, had claimed another victim. Generose covered the coffee table with a piece of beige fabric and brought out a stack of small plates and a fistful of forks from the kitchen. The boys followed with the food: a large plastic bowl full of steaming rice and smaller ceramic bowls containing helpings of warm cassava, beans, potatoes, and stewed greens. Generose pressed Play on the VCR, and the screen came to life with the blurry images of a Catholic choir from Congo, singing hymns outdoors against changing backdrops of mountains and green forests.

Generose, who spoke Swahili, some French, and Kirundi—the language of Bujumbura and western Burundi— knew only a few words of English. Alex, fifteen and the oldest, understood English, but spoke with a thick Burundian accent that, combined with his deepening and sometimes cracking voice, made him hard to understand sometimes. Sensing this, perhaps, Alex was shy and quiet and spoke mainly in Swahili to his family. Bienvenue—Bien or Bienve to his family—was two years younger, and had picked up the new language more quickly than Alex. Luma had gotten Bien into a nearby charter school that focused on immigrants and refugees. The extra help the school offered had improved Bien's English quickly. He spoke with less of an accent than Alex, and though he struggled with writing and reading, he liked to make jokes, and that gave him the drive to improve his spoken English. When he got hung up searching for a word or phrase, Bien would lower his chin, place his open palm on the crown of his head, and rotate it in small quick circles, the same motion, I learned later, that Generose had used to soothe him when he cried as a child.

Ive, who was seven, spoke English fluently and with no accent. His favorite TV show was *The Simpsons,* and he spoke with a knowing tone that sounded a lot like Bart Simpson's. As the best English speaker in the family, Ive often had to answer the phone and speak with Americans—the landlord, billing agents from the phone and power companies—who were decades older than he was.

Generose had managed to keep a part-time job as a stocker at a local drugstore for a while, but since giving birth to Alyah six months before, she had been unemployed. She had no money, she said. Alyah's father, in Canada now and without immigration papers to get into the United States, helped out as much as he could by sending money, and a well-to-do Atlanta woman who helped refugee families as a volunteer with the International Rescue Committee donated groceries and helped Generose make ends meet while she looked for a job. But working would require Generose to find day care for Alyah, creating a new expense. To come out ahead after child-care costs, Generose figured she would have to find work that paid thirteen or fourteen dollars an hour. If such work existed in Atlanta for unskilled applicants who spoke no English, Generose had yet to find it.

Rent for the family's two-bedroom apartment was $650. Power and phone bills amounted to nearly $200 a month. Food was a relatively cheap but not inconsequential expense; Generose bought her rice in bulk, in large, fifty-pound plastic sacks from the DeKalb County farmers' market, just down the road. She was open to a job at night, she said; that way the boys could babysit Alyah when they returned from school while she worked, and she could sleep and stay with the baby during the day.

It showed how desperate Generose had become that she was willing to leave her six-month-old daughter in the care of her three sons, ages seven, thirteen, and fifteen. While in a refugee camp in Mozambique, Generose had lost a daughter to a domestic accident. The girl had accidentally knocked over a pot of boiling potatoes and was badly scalded, and Generose, too poor to afford a ride to a hospital, was left to wrap her daughter's burns with leaves. For a time it seemed the girl might be fine, but eventually her wounds became worse, and she died, just nine years old. Generose was constantly shooing her younger children out of the kitchen, and allowed only Alex, the eldest, to cook on the stove. She feared leaving her children alone. But she had to find a way to provide for them.

Generose hadn't thought that living in the United States would force her to decide between working and watching her children. Like many refugees in Clarkston, she had put so much of her energy and hope into getting out of a refugee camp that she hadn't thought much about what life might be like after she arrived in a new country. "I thought America would be paradise," Generose said, through Bien.

"We thought America would be like this," Alex said,

pretending to be a magician with a wand and flicking it at the table.

"Soda!" he said, then, flicking the wand again: "Food!"

Bien, Generose, and Ive guffawed along with Alex.

"No worry, no worry," Generose said in her sparse English, raising her hands. "God very, very good."

13

Trying Again

Tryouts for the possible revival of the Under Fifteens were set for Monday afternoon on the sandy field behind Indian Creek Elementary. Kanue, Mandela, and Natnael had come through—new faces were arriving from the footpaths through the surrounding woods—though there had been some confusion about the start time. The boys had told everyone to show up at five-thirty p.m. but told their coach to show up at six p.m., then forgot about the difference. So for half an hour the boys stretched, jogged, and passed a ball around, all the while watching for Luma's yellow Beetle. Perhaps, someone said aloud, she had changed her mind.

As the boys waited, members of the two other Fugee teams began to show up as well, to see what sort of talent Kanue, Mandela, and Natnael had found. Word that something was up with the Fugees seemed to have spread to even the neighborhood kids who didn't play soccer; boys and girls who would have run across the field in the middle of practice gathered quietly beside the track and climbed atop the big orange and blue jungle gym to watch.

At five minutes to six, the yellow Volkswagen pulled into the lot. Luma got out, opened the trunk, and took out a mesh bag full of soccer balls. She heaved the bag over her shoulder and made her way to the field.

Luma looked at the young men who had turned out. There were six familiar faces; four from the current Under Fifteens—Kanue, Natnael, Mandela, and Bien's older brother, Alex—and two boys who had come out for practices with the Fugees in the past. The rest were unknowns. Notably absent was Fornatee; when the other boys had called him, he had explained that he wanted to play for the Under Fifteens if Luma gave the team another chance. But he felt strongly that he had tried out once before and shouldn't have to try out again. It was an insult, he said.

Luma gathered the newcomers, asked their names, and wrote them down on a sheet of paper. Then she divided the group into two teams and told them she planned simply to watch them play. As the boys took the field, Luma noticed that one boy was wearing sandals. She called him over and placed her foot alongside his: they were close to the same size. Luma kicked off the black Puma soccer shoes she wore each day to practice and offered them to the boy, who stepped out of his sandals and slipped the shoes on. Sock-footed, Luma sat on the ground and watched the scrimmage in silence.

"It feels like our first season," she said finally. "There's no base for the team. If we could practice five days a week we might be able to make it—"

She cut herself off. With two other teams to coach, that wasn't possible. If Luma decided to reinstate the Fifteens, they'd have perhaps three practices before their first game. She'd be lucky if her players learned one another's names. She had her concerns too about some of the new kids; she didn't know yet who they were, or if they were the sort of boys she wanted in her program. And Luma feared that by going ahead with the season, she might be setting her players up for failure.

"I don't know," she said. "I just don't know."

Luma studied the players. Kanue was leading the scrimmage, calling out to his teammates, urging them to pass, and sprinting for each free ball. The new players responded. There was a pair of Somali Bantu brothers, Hamdu and Jeylani Muganga, who were relentless on defense. Mandela charged his way through traffic, using his large frame to shield the ball, and scored a goal. Natnael flicked a series of clever passes across the field to players he'd never met before. The boys were playing as if they were trying to will their team back into existence.

Luma watched intently, making notes next to the players' names on the sheet of paper she held. She drew a soccer field on the back and began to write names in positions: The Mugangas were quick and determined; Luma wrote their names on the back line, on defense, and put Alex in between. She put Kanue at center midfielder, Natnael at left mid, and Mandela at striker. There was a quick-footed young Bosnian player named Muamer. He was an excellent ball handler, even though he was raw and seemed never to pass. Luma put him at right forward. She wrote other names down, erased them, and wrote them down again at other positions until the sheet of paper was a jumble of names and smudges.

After an hour or so, Luma blew her whistle and called everyone in. The boys waited for Luma to speak.

"Out of the sixteen players here today I have coached six," she told them. "So only six of you know how I am as a coach, and only six know what kind of players I expect. And only six know what rules I have.

"If we go in with this team," she continued, "we're probably going to lose the majority of our games. We might win one or two if we're lucky."

One of the newcomers groaned in disagreement.

"Are you guys going to be okay going into a season and losing most of your games?" she asked.

There was no response.

"You're playing teams that have been together five years," she said. "We're not going to play this weekend. You play the weekend after—you will have been together one week. So five years against one week."

Luma pointed out that they'd have just three practices to get their team together.

Kanue spoke up. They could get an extra practice in early Saturday morning, he said. The other kids nodded—they'd be there.

"We can do this," Kanue said.

"If you still want it, then I'll see you Thursday at five," Luma said. "And if you don't—don't show up Thursday.

"Practices are not going to be easy," she added. "You're going to be running more than the other teams, kicking the ball a lot more. And I'm not going to be nice. So if you thought I was mean these past two weeks . . ."

Luma let that thought hang in the air for a moment, and then turned to walk from the field.

Kanue dropped his head in relief. His team was alive. He was going to make sure everyone was there on Thursday afternoon, on time. He also planned to talk to Coach about that extra practice on Saturday morning. But for now he simply wanted to let her know what was on his mind, and he did so quietly, when no one else was around.

"I told her I appreciate her," Kanue said later. "I told her thanks, and that we were going to do everything to follow the rules and give her the respect she deserves."

14

The Fifteens Fight

There was plenty of raw talent among the group of boys who had come out for the second edition of the Fugees' Under Fifteens, but they were a diverse group. The boys came from Liberia, Kosovo, Sudan, Somalia, Burundi, Bosnia, Ethiopia, and Afghanistan, and while most spoke some English, they had little in common. With just nine days to go before their first game, Luma figured her best shot at getting this group of boys to bond was to make them face a great challenge together. After two standard practices that focused on the basics of passing and ball handling, she scheduled a scrimmage between the new Under Fifteens and their counterparts on the Under Seventeen team. The Fifteens were likely to be beaten, which was the point; their reaction to playing a much better opponent would tell Luma a lot about their chances as a team. If the Under Fifteens lost their cool against the older Fugees, she figured, they stood little chance against the tougher competition to come.

In truth, she wasn't sure they could pull it off. Mandela, one of the three anchors of the team, along with Natnael and Kanue, was worrying her. Although he'd helped his friends find new players, at the practices following tryouts he was quiet and angry. Mandela was still mad that his friend Prince wasn't on the team because of the hair rule, which he thought was stupid. And now Fornatee, his other close friend on the team, hadn't shown up for the new round of tryouts. Of his clique, Mandela was now alone on the team, which included Bosnians, Kosovars, and Somali Bantu kids he'd never met before. That wasn't what Mandela had signed up for. He seemed to have little interest in getting to know the new players. Before practice, he hid within his headphones and juggled a ball, not speaking to anyone. During practice, he snapped at kids who made bad passes or who couldn't set him up for a shot during scrimmages. Sometimes Mandela simply wandered off in the middle of practice, once for no reason and another time to join a pickup game of older players from the neighborhood at the far end of the field.

Luma sensed that Mandela was upset and disappointed that his friends weren't playing. She decided to ride out his moods, hoping he would come around.

Fornatee Tarpeh had heard about the scrimmage from the kids in his apartment complex. Though he had not shown up at the second tryouts or at either practice, Fornatee thought scrimmage day was the right time to approach Coach Luma and ask to rejoin the team. He knew he was talented and figured the Under Fifteens needed someone like him up front.

Standing on the field on scrimmage day, waiting to speak to his coach, Fornatee said he had skipped the second tryouts as a matter of pride. "I wasn't going to come to tryouts," he said, "because I *tried out.* I love playing soccer," he added as he waited for Coach. "I love playing with my friends, but my friends aren't here. It's like you break up with your family. And this is why: don't nobody want to cut their hair. I want to play on the team, but I want to play on the team with my friends."

I asked Fornatee what it felt like to be off Luma's team.

"I'm not *off* the team," he snapped. "She hasn't called me, and I haven't called her. So in my opinion, I'm still on the team."

A few minutes later, Luma arrived. Members of the Under Fifteens and Seventeens were warming up when she walked onto the field past Fornatee, without making eye contact. Luma blew her whistle and told the two teams to gather at opposite ends of the field.

"She's more than a coach—that's why," Fornatee said, almost to himself. "She's a great person. I'm going to go over there and tell her, 'That's my team.'"

Fornatee hesitated. I asked him if he was nervous about talking to Coach. He laughed anxiously, then composed himself.

"Nah—I'm not nervous," he said.

A moment later, Fornatee made his way toward Luma. She was standing in a huddle of Under Fifteen players, assigning them their positions. Fornatee tried to blend into the group as if he expected to get a position.

"Fornatee," Luma said when she saw him, "go away."

Fornatee was startled. He froze as the other players turned to look at him.

"Coach, can I talk to you after?" he asked.

"Yes—go away," Luma said before continuing with her position assignments. Fornatee walked back to the jungle gym, where Prince and some of his other friends had gathered to watch the scrimmage. He would watch and wait, and try to persuade Coach to take him back.

The Seventeens were not just older and more mature than the Fifteens; they were much more talented. They were led by a talkative and self-confident Iraqi refugee named Peshawa Hamad and a quiet, graceful Sudanese player named Shamsoun Dikori, whose younger brothers, Idwar and Robin, played on the Under Thirteens. Luma had no doubt who would win the scrimmage, but she wanted to see how the Fifteens would react to the challenge. She handed out red mesh jersey pullovers to the Fifteens; the Seventeens wore white. Luma designated the two chain-link baseball backstops on the field as goals. She blew the whistle, and soon a white cloud of dust began to rise from the scuffling feet of the two sides.

The Fifteens displayed a new energy and determination, and took control of the ball. On an early run, Mandela set up Muamer, the new, mustachioed Bosnian forward, with a touch pass off the back of his foot, but Muamer missed the shot.

"Man!" Mandela shouted in frustration.

Moments later, Peshawa slithered through the Fifteens' defenses and fired a shot that clanged into the chain-link fence of the backstop.

The Seventeens were up 1–0.

The Fifteens didn't give up. Soon Mandela dribbled through a seam in the Seveteens' defense, got a clear view of the goal, and fired a perfect shot: *clang!* The Fifteens had tied it 1–1. Luma blew the whistle for halftime. She summoned the Fifteens. "You're outhustling them—keep it up," she told them.

On the Seventeens' side of the field, Peshawa had grown angry: he had no intention of getting shown up by the younger team.

"Wake up!" he said to his teammates. "They only have Mandela. Shut that down and they don't have anything. Control the middle. These players—they're nothing. Let's finish it off!"

In the second half, the Seventeens took advantage of their size and experience. Their passes were crisp, and they chipped their way downfield, using their elbows to control the movements of the younger, smaller team. Again Peshawa juked around the Fifteens' midfielders and a toddler who had wandered onto the field, then tapped the ball around Hamdu Muganga, one of the two Somali Bantu brothers who had joined the Fifteens on defense. Peshawa scored; 2–1, the Seventeens now led.

A few minutes later, Kanue was dribbling downfield and had just passed the ball when one of the older players took him out with a vicious tackle. Kanue rolled forward violently on his right shoulder and tumbled to a stop in the dust. He looked up for a whistle, but there was none. Luma was letting them play. Kanue was furious. He set his sights on the young man who had tackled him, and with the ball clear across the field, Kanue slid into his ankles, cleats up—a move that would have drawn a red card in a regulation contest.

"Hey!" Luma shouted. "Kanue! Take a lap."

When Luma blew her whistle a few minutes later, the final score was 3–2 in favor of the Seventeens. Luma waved the Fifteens over.

"Fifteens, you played a decent game," she told them. "Kanue, if I see you lose your temper again, you're off the team. They're going to foul you in a game and you'll get red-carded." Kanue shook his head in disappointment with himself. He knew he had made an error, the kind that could put the whole team in jeopardy. Coach had let him off easy with a lap.

After practice, Luma had concerns: Kanue's outburst had been troubling, and she wasn't happy that Mandela was lashing out at his new teammates when they made mistakes. But the Fifteens' effort had been impressive. They hadn't quit when they fell behind. They wanted to win.

There was one more order of business before Luma could wrap up her day. She had agreed to hear out Fornatee's case for why he ought to be allowed back on the team. Luma turned and looked toward the jungle gym, where Fornatee had been watching the scrimmage with Prince and the others. But the boys were no longer there. At some point during the scrimmage, they'd walked off, and, in Fornatee's case, away from the team for good.

Luma gathered the soccer balls into a mesh sack, which

she slung over her shoulder and carried toward her car. The parking lot was teeming with young men who had come to hang around the basketball court, some of whom were drinking. She kept her head down and walked straight to her Beetle. She opened the hatchback and heaved the sack of balls into the backseat. Truth be told, she was growing tired of the whole scene at Indian Creek—the chaos on the field as well as the menacing crowd in the parking lot.

There was a safer place for the Fugees to play: Armistead Field in Milam Park. Besides offering the luxury of grass, Armistead Field was set away from the flow of pedestrians in and out of the apartment complexes. The field was in a hollow, surrounded by chain-link fence. Clarkston police cars frequently patrolled the park. The thought that such a perfect field was sitting unused made Luma angry. She resolved to do something about it.

The next day, Luma got in her yellow Volkswagen and drove to City Hall to ask Mayor Swaney to let the Fugees use the field. Swaney was in his office when Luma arrived, and agreed to speak with her. She spoke calmly; she didn't want the mayor to get upset. Luma pointed out that her program kept kids off the streets after school, at no cost to the city. It was exactly the sort of program, she argued, that Clarkston should support. The field in Milam Park was completely unused; it seemed little to ask that the Fugees be allowed to practice there four days a week.

Lee Swaney took it all in. Her appeal put him in a tough spot. He'd catch hell from some of the longtime Clarkston residents, especially those who lived around Milam Park, if he gave a group of refugees free run of the place. At the same time, the mayor had no appetite for negative publicity.

Swaney told Luma that he couldn't give her permission to use the empty field, but that she was free to make her case to the Clarkston City Council, which met on the first Tuesday of each month. As it happened, the October meeting was just five days away. Luma planned to attend.

15

Go Fugees!

On the morning of the Under Fifteens' first game after their suspension, Luma woke up in her small two-bedroom apartment in Decatur, hurried down a short hallway to the bathroom, hunched over the toilet, and threw up.

Luma had never become sick before a game until now. Her nerves were frayed. She was terrified that her team might get humiliated by their opponents. Luma understood she was dealing with a group of boys with little self-esteem to spare. Kanue, Natnael, and especially Mandela had put their hopes and energy into this new version of their team, and Luma wondered if she was setting them up for failure by keeping the season alive. She didn't know what she would say or do to comfort them if they got blown out.

The game was set for Ebster Field on a late-September

Saturday. A cooling breeze rolled over the foothills east of Atlanta. It was perfect soccer weather. The white YMCA bus arrived on time, and to Luma's relief, a full roster of players jogged onto the field. The Fugees ran laps to warm up, Kanue in the lead. He led his teammates through a stretching routine and then had them take the pitch to practice penalty shots. The opposing team was the AFC Lightning from Fayetteville, Georgia, a mostly white middle-class suburb south of Atlanta. The Lightning came from a well-established soccer program with a history of sending teams to both state and national championships. The players on this particular Lightning team were big, and looked on average a good two years older than the Fugees. Their coach barked commands in a booming voice that rang off the brick buildings of the housing projects across the street. The Lightning wore red and gold and traveled with parents, friends, and siblings, who had made the fifty-minute trip to Decatur and set up camp on the sideline across from the Lightning bench. The Fugees had exactly three fans: a couple who occasionally volunteered to help Luma with tutoring and transportation, and a young Liberian named Tito, who had been recruited late by a Liberian player named Osman and who hoped someday to make the team.

Luma called her players in. Her pregame instructions were spare: no cussing, and no tackling from behind. She didn't want any players getting carded or losing their cool. The Fugees nodded.

"Are you ready?" she asked them.

"Yes!" came the reply.

Luma extended her arm and her players formed a circle

around her and stacked their hands on hers. She counted to three and the boys responded with a chant of "Go Fugees!"

The Fugees began the game tentatively. They turned the ball over early on clumsy passes, and then let the Lightning sneak past for a pair of early shots that went wide. Luma subbed her players frequently, to keep them rested and to see which lineups worked best. Not ten minutes into the game, a Lightning player settled a pass on the wing and sprinted down the line past Kanue and into open space. From twenty yards out, he pivoted and quickly took the shot, catching the Fugees' goalie flat-footed. The ball sailed beneath the crossbar and into the net. The Fugees were down 1–0.

Kanue urged his teammates to keep their spirits up. Soon the Fugees made a run down the right side, but Muamer drew the linesman's flag for being offside. The Fugees made another go; Muamer was called offside again, to groans from his teammates. Kanue didn't snap at Muamer; he simply gestured with his hand to encourage his new teammate to stay onside, to be patient.

Soon the Fugees made another run; this time Mandela took off down the right line. He powered through the Lightning defenders and worked the ball back toward the middle of the field before blasting a shot that hit the right post and bounced in: 1–1.

As the half wore on, the Fugees charged once, twice, and then a third time, at one point racing down the field at a full sprint, like kids chasing an ice cream truck. Finally, they were getting somewhere. Kanue floated a pass downfield to Mandela, who traded passes with Hamdu as they attacked the Lightning defense. When the defense converged,

Mandela flicked the ball to Sebajden, a wiry Kosovar midfielder, who volleyed the shot: goal. At the half, the Fugees led 2–1.

At halftime, Luma tried not to let her relief show. She gathered her players in a corner of the field and quickly ran through her observations.

"Listen up," she told them. "You're playing well, but it's getting sloppy. What they do is get the ball and either cross it or switch the field and they overlap. They do the same thing over and over and over again. Don't let them do it. Don't let them do it."

Her players nodded. They understood.

"The midfielders need to get in there and squeeze them out before they can cross it in. Okay? Don't give them any crosses, because they could finish them off.

"Next thing: Mandela—they're going to mark you this half," she said. The strategy now, she told him, was to head in to the box, draw the defenders, and kick the ball out wide to the open player. After doing that a couple of times, she told him, he should take the shot himself. But not until then.

"A good soccer player is not going to let them know what he's going to do every time," she said. ·

Mandela nodded. Kanue tapped him gently on the back. They could win this.

"You guys have been doing great," Luma told her players. "When you've been going in for the attack, there's like eight of you charging through. They're not going to be able to defend eight of you. Okay? You need to keep it up at that level. All right? It's two to one. We need two more. It's your first game. You need to set the tone for the season today."

* * *

The Fugees took the field in the second half with a new energy and confidence. The Lightning marked Mandela, as Luma had predicted. In frustration, Mandela pushed off, drawing a yellow card. Kanue patted the air with his palms, gesturing to Mandela to calm down. Mandela nodded, seeming to remember what Coach had said. On the next trip down the field, Mandela powered through the hulking Lightning midfielders and dribbled toward the box. The defense collapsed around him, just as his coach had told him they would. Mandela jabbed a pass out on the wing to Muamer, who was open. He tapped the ball, altering its angle and freezing the goalie. The ball rolled clear and into the net: 3–1, Fugees.

With twelve minutes to go, the Lightning drew within a goal, on a penalty kick. Time was winding down, and the Fugees were getting tired. Kanue encouraged them to keep fighting; Coach had told them to get two more—they had one to go. Moments later, Mandela broke free again up the middle of the field. This time he charged the box, and when the defenders marked their men on the wings, he followed his coach's advice again and took the shot himself: goal. Tito, the Liberian recruit, and the two volunteers shouted in celebration. It was 4–2, Fugees.

The final minutes of the game were desperate and dangerous. Kanue caught a finger to the eye and crumpled to the ground, only to rise moments later in anger. Luma shouted to him to keep himself under control; he took a deep breath and walked away. The Fugees were tired. The Lightning made a run, took a shot, and appeared to score, but the linesman raised his flag to signify offside. Angry now, they made another run, and set up the overlap and cross on the right side—the very sequence Luma had warned her players to shut down. Kanue called out to his teammates to cover the overlap, but it was too late. The Lightning forward was in the open; he leaned into his shot and blasted the ball into the upper-right corner of the net. It was 4–3. The Lightning had seized the momentum. Their parents and coach were urging them on. There was a sense that the Fugees had run out of energy.

"No, guys!" Tito called from the sideline. "Don't let it happen!"

The Lightning would have their chance to tie in the final moments, when Hamdu Muganga, now on defense for the Fugees, was called for a foul at the top of the penalty box. The Lightning were awarded a free kick from fifteen yards out. A lean, blond striker set up to take the kick. His teammates lined up on the left and right of the goal. He gave the signal, and his teammates charged just as he connected with all his might. The ball sailed on a head-high line drive toward a mass of bodies in front of the goal. Unable to see the ball, the Fugees' goalie was frozen. From the midst of the scrum, a light blue jersey leaped into the air; it was Kanue. He cocked his neck and thrust his head into the speeding ball. There was a violent thud, and the ball shot back toward the lanky striker who had kicked it, sailing over his head and bouncing into the empty space at midfield. The ball was still rolling when the referee blew his whistle—once, twice, and again—to signal the end of the game. The Fugees had won.

Luma dropped her head in relief. Her players, some of them still strangers to each other, were high-fiving and shouting joyfully at the sky as they ran toward her on the bench. They seemed as surprised as she did. Luma raised her head, pulled her shoulders back, and smiled for the first time in two weeks.

"You guys floored me," she told her players when they had settled down enough to hear her speak. The Fugees broke into applause, for one another and for their coach.

"To tell you the truth, I didn't think you guys were going to come through today," Luma said finally. "But you played a beautiful game."

16

Gunshots

The gunshots sounded at first like small firecrackers rather than anything dangerous. They came one, then another, and another, echoing between the buildings of the apartment complexes behind Indian Creek Elementary at about ten-forty Sunday morning. When the shooting was finished, Tito, the Liberian whom Osman had recruited to the Under Fifteens and who had cheered the Fugees on to victory the day before, was covered in blood, shot in the face.

The exact circumstances of the shooting were murky. A few details were given to police by witnesses. Tito and some fellow Liberians were walking up the street when they ran into an African American teenager they knew, walking with his mother and her boyfriend. An argument ensued. The kids on the team heard that the argument had to do with territory

135

and gangs. The shooter was in a gang of American kids; Tito and his fellow Liberians, who identified themselves as members of a gang called the Africans, were walking on the wrong turf. The American teenager whipped out a small-caliber pistol and began shooting. Everyone ran, including the shooter, who dashed back to his apartment.

When the police arrived a few minutes later, they found the American kid's mother at the scene of the shooting, picking up the shells that had discharged from her son's weapon. She claimed her son had been in their apartment all morning, asleep; but eyewitnesses to the shooting identified the sixteen-year-old as the shooter, and DeKalb County police officers handcuffed him and loaded him into the backseat of their black-and-gray squad car. Tito himself was lucky: the bullet had crashed into his chin and ripped through his jaw. A little lower, and it would have cut through his neck, spinal cord, or carotid arteries; a few inches higher, and it might have entered his brain. Tito, on this day, would survive.

Luma was shaken by the news. She worried about her other players. Rival gang members knew that Tito had been practicing with the Fugees, with his close friend Osman, and everyone in Clarkston knew exactly where and when the Fugees practiced. Luma feared gang members might show up to try to take revenge for their friend who had been arrested. She canceled practices and got the word out to her players not to show up at the field at Indian Creek until further notice. She drew a hard line with Tito and Osman as well. None of the Fugees had heard of a gang called the Africans, and many thought Tito had been bluffing to frighten the

American boy when he claimed to be in such a gang. Luma wasn't sure, but even pretending to be part of a gang was enough for her. Tito and Osman were to have nothing to do with her soccer program ever again.

For Luma, it was difficult to imagine ever feeling safe on the field at Indian Creek Elementary. The field was next door to the apartment complex where the shooter lived, which Luma now knew was also considered the territory of a street gang in conflict with some of her own (now former) players. The field at Indian Creek was a free-for-all in the afternoons; there were no fences around the property, and neighborhood teenagers were constantly popping out of the surrounding woods. It would be impossible to sort out a stranger who was simply taking a shortcut by walking across the field from one with bad intentions. Luma had promised her players' parents that she would keep them safe; she wasn't sure she could keep that promise at Indian Creek. On Tuesday night, Luma would have a chance to improve things for her team if she could convince the Clarkston City Council to let her use the city's field in Milam Park.

17

The "Soccer People"

On the first Tuesday night in October, Luma went to City Hall to make her case for the Fugees' use of the field in the town park. She had a lot riding on the council's decision. The fields at Clarkston High School and at nearby Georgia Perimeter College were booked for the fall. The Clarkston Community Center was no longer an option due to a rift between the center and the YMCA, and the field behind Indian Creek was too dangerous given Tito's shooting, Luma believed. She refused to put her players at risk. Her best bet if the council turned her down was to find a parking lot someplace where the boys could play, or else to cancel practices altogether.

The meeting was called to order and began with the Pledge of Allegiance. Committee reports were asked for and delivered. The council then moved on to the people's business.

Luma rose and approached the lectern. She spoke in a soft, meek voice and introduced herself as the head of a soccer program for Clarkston's youth.

"We'd like to request the use of Armistead Field as our field to practice on, Monday through Thursday, from five till sunset," she said.

"Why?" a councilwoman asked.

"The field at Indian Creek Elementary is all gravel," said Luma. "It's also not controlled. Anyone can go there and play, so unsupervised kids are out there playing. Unsupervised adults are out there playing. And it's not a healthy environment for kids."

A barrage of questions followed: What would it cost the town? How old were the boys? Were they local? Would they be supervised? What kind of equipment would they be using? What about insurance? Luma said she would always supervise; the team would supply its own equipment; the program would be insured; the players were all local.

"Are these mixed teams for both boys and girls?" another councilwoman asked.

"No, it's just boys right now," Luma said.

"Just *boys*," the woman said. An awkward silence followed, broken eventually by Mayor Swaney.

"This lady came and talked to me about using the lower end of Armistead Field—using the end for soccer," he said. "She knows that you don't play soccer on a baseball field. And we got the lower end of this field that we do not use and have not used. And the only time it was used was when grown people—grown soccer people—came in there with cleats and everything else, and were tearing the field up."

The council members leaned forward to look at the mayor to see where he was going with all this.

"So, you know," he said finally, "I don't see anything wrong with this lady using the lower end of Armistead Field, doing a little soccer to get our kids off the streets. How does the council feel about letting this lady use the lower end of Armistead Field for a trial period, and let's see what happens?"

Swaney's proposal changed the energy in the room. The council's questions became gentler. They talked among themselves and agreed that six months sounded like a reasonable amount of time for a trial period.

There was a motion, and a second.

The motion passed unanimously. Luma nodded in thanks and stifled a smile. The Fugees, for now at least, had a home.

18

Playing on Grass

"What makes people join a gang?" Luma asked the boys.

"Race," said one.

"Money."

"Protection."

"To be cool."

"To be men."

"What makes a gang different from the Fugees?" Luma asked.

"They fight."

"They shoot each other."

"Once you're part of a gang, you can't get away."

"In a gang, you have to do whatever they want. Otherwise, if you don't do it, you get shot."

After Tito's shooting and her meeting with the

city council, Luma called separate meetings of the Under Thirteens and Fifteens, which she held in a classroom at Indian Creek Elementary during practice time. At Luma's invitation, the town police chief met with the younger team while Luma addressed the Fifteens. It was clear that the Fugees knew more about gangs than Luma might have hoped.

"How many here would know where to join a gang in their neighborhood?" she asked.

"I would," said one boy.

Luma called Kanue to the front of the room, pulled an iPod out of her pocket, and offered to give it to him if he agreed to carry something for her. Kanue hesitated. The boys responded with nervous laughter.

"They give you money—they say, 'Oh, here's five bucks, walk this across the street for me,'" Luma said. "They say, 'I know Kanue wants an iPod.' Or 'Mandela wants a new pair of Air Jordans.'

"Why do people do that? Because they're the ones who don't want to get caught," Luma said. "They want you to do the dangerous work. And once you do it once, once you do it twice, you're in their gang. You're a part of them. And you're not going to get out. Okay? Because they would rather kill you than have you get out and maybe tell the police."

Luma asked the boys what sorts of things they could say if someone offered them money or an iPod to carry something.

"I would say, 'Give me the iPod first,'" one kid said. The boys laughed.

"What else could you say?" Luma asked.

"I'm sorry, I'm going the other way."

"You said if you do it, like, three or four times you're in," said another kid. "So Tito did it three or four times?"

"I don't know if Tito ran drugs," Luma said. "I don't know if Tito joined a gang to be cool, or for protection, or because he didn't want to walk down the street and get jumped."

The boys frowned. This last point was one they could relate to. Walking through the complexes around town could be tough, since you never knew when you might be treading on someone else's turf. Who wouldn't want protection? Luma sensed the boys' discomfort.

"If I got beat up, I would want someone helping me out— to beat them up," she said. The boys laughed.

"I would," Luma said. "But what other ways could I look at it? What other things could I do?"

The boys called out in response: You could tell someone. You could tell the police. You could take another route.

"Right," Luma said finally. "And if you keep getting beat up on the same road, take a different road."

Luma let the message sink in for a few moments. The classroom quieted, and several of the boys lowered their gazes to the floor in a quiet signal that they understood: if you keep getting beat up on the same road, take a different road.

Luma had an announcement that proved she planned to practice what she had been preaching. The Fugees, she said, were finished playing soccer at Indian Creek Elementary. Beginning on Tuesday, she said, practicing would take place across town at Milam Park. The field was flat, she told them, with grass and no other soccer teams. Practicing there would let them play without distractions or fear for their safety. But it came with responsibility.

"You are the first soccer team to use that field," she said. "So you have to set an example so other people can use that field for soccer."

Everyone would be expected to pick up trash in the park so no one in town blamed the Fugees for any mess. To get to the field, the boys would have to walk past houses of older Clarkston residents in the neighborhood behind the library and community center. Luma told them she'd better not hear any reports of yelling or cussing or turning over trash cans. And no one was to go on the field until Luma was there.

"I need you guys to be responsible and respectful," she said.

"I know where the field is," one of the kids said. "But I'm not sure if I can walk there."

"You don't walk, you don't practice," Luma said. "Nobody here is in perfect shape. You all could use the exercise.

"Nobody has an excuse not to get to that field," she added. "You don't want to play, don't show up. That's the field we're going to be playing on, okay? We're not going to be playing on this field—ever again."

The boys could hardly believe their eyes when they showed up for their first practices in Milam Park. Compared with the dust bowl at Indian Creek Elementary, Armistead Field was perfect: a thick blanket of soft green grass covered the playing surface and scratched the players' backs when they splayed out for sit-ups and stretches. The field was surrounded on three sides by tall trees draped in a tangle of vines. On the fourth side was a steep hill with a crumbling set of concrete steps. The hill offered a stadium-like view of the field below.

A chain-link fence formed an oval boundary around the field, forcing visitors on their way to the playgrounds and picnic tables on the far side of Milam Park to take a detour around the playing area. The Fugees truly had a home field to themselves.

The beauty of the Fugees' new home was so extraordinary that it almost seemed like a joke. At an early practice, as the boys were scrimmaging, a gaggle of geese took flight from a pond on the other side of the woods. They flapped and honked noisily as they flew low over Armistead Field, startling the Under Thirteens, who then began laughing at the idea that they had been spooked by a flock of birds. At another practice, the Under Fifteens had gathered in a circle at midfield to stretch, when they heard noises in the woods—snapping twigs and the crushing of dry leaves. As the sound grew louder, the puzzled members of the Fifteens quieted and turned their heads in the direction of the hill alongside the field, just as a small herd of deer wandered into the clearing. The boys could hardly believe their eyes.

"We should chase them," Hamdu Muganga whispered eventually to his teammates as they peered at the grazing animals.

"Nah, Hamdu," said a lanky Sudanese midfielder named Kuur. "We're not in Africa anymore."

PART THREE
Full Circle

19

Who Are the Kings?

The Fugees all had their own soccer idols—David Beckham, Ronaldo, Ronaldinho, and the Ivorian Didier Drogba—the stars they wanted to play like on the field. Qendrim Bushi's soccer idol was his grandfather, once a famous goalkeeper at the highest level of play in Kosovo, and later, a well-known referee and the author of an Albanian-language soccer rule book. The Bushi family kept a tattered copy of the rule book in their apartment just outside Clarkston, one of a few things they had managed to bring with them to the United States, and one of Qendrim's most prized possessions.

"He was very famous in my country," Qendrim explained as he thumbed through the book one afternoon. "He used to be one of the best goalkeepers in Kosovo, and everybody wanted to be like him."

Qendrim—everyone on the Fugees called him "KWIN-drum" but his family pronounced it "CHIN-drim"—was a tiny but talented midfielder for the Under Thirteen Fugees. He had narrow eyes that often seemed lit with a secret, as if he alone were in on some long-running joke that the rest of the world would come to appreciate later on. He had pencil-like legs that packed surprising power, and he was a student of the game, which his father also played. He studied his grandfather's rule book and talked strategy with his dad. Soccer was in Qendrim's blood.

The Bushi family came from Kacanik, an Albanian town of twenty-eight thousand in the mountains of southern Kosovo, not far from the border with Macedonia. Qendrim's father, Xhalal—pronounced Ja-LAL—owned two small grocery stores there with his brother and father, one of which was located in the lower floor of the Bushis' home. Together the stores provided the family with a comfortable life in Kacanik, until ethnic violence tore their homeland apart. Kacanik was one of many towns in southern Kosovo that became battlegrounds in the 1990s in the struggle between the Serb-dominated Yugoslav army of Slobodan Milošević, which was trying to assert Serbian control over the mostly Albanian-inhabited region, and the Kosovo Liberation Army (KLA), the ethnically Albanian militia that was fighting for independence. Civilians in Kacanik were hurt by both sides in the conflict. KLA soldiers had put sometimes violent pressure on fellow Albanians to flee Kacanik for refugee camps in Macedonia, with the aim of provoking sympathy from the international community and—they hoped—a military response.

NATO bombing, which was ordered by then-President

Bill Clinton and which would eventually prompt Serb forces to withdraw from Kosovo, began on March 24, 1999. In response, Milošević's army unleashed a wave of destruction and brutality on some sixty towns and cities in Kosovo. Kacanik's time came three days after the bombing began, on March 27, when Milošević's forces ransacked the town's commercial district, stealing food and valuables from residents and cleaning off the shelves of grocery stores, including those owned by the Bushis. The Serbian army holed up in Kacanik, but two weeks later, on April 9, a swarm of KLA militiamen attacked the Serbian soldiers there. The battle, which took place largely on Kacanik's main street, left seventeen dead. The next day, Serbian soldiers came to take revenge for the attack. As they approached, many Kacanik residents fled along a canyon path that ran beside a stream.

Eyewitnesses said that Serbian police drove an armored vehicle equipped with a twin-barreled antiaircraft cannon through town, shooting all the way. Sharpshooters fired on those fleeing through the canyon. There were bodies everywhere. The summer after the fighting ended, NATO troops discovered a mass grave containing the remains of ninety-three people just outside Kacanik. Some were KLA soldiers, but most were town residents, identified from scraps of clothing they'd been wearing the day they were last seen alive.

Xhalal Bushi had managed to get his wife and children to Macedonia before the fighting, but he and his brother had gone back to Kacanik to look after their homes and stores. Their presence didn't help; their stores and homes were still destroyed by the Serbian army.

"My house is burned," Xhalal said, sitting on a sofa in his apartment outside Clarkston. "They put some bomb in it and destroyed everything." He flung his hands in the air: "Boom!" Xhalal and his brother fled Kacanik on foot and walked for two days over mountains toward Macedonia. They drank water from streams as they walked, and went without food, until they were found by Macedonian soldiers, who placed them in a refugee camp. Xhalal was reunited with Qendrim, his wife, and his daughter, and together they lived in the camp for three months, awaiting placement by the United Nations High Commissioner for Refugees.

The Bushis were grateful when they learned they had been granted asylum by the United States, but the news was bittersweet. Xhalal's extended family was broken up, sent to a variety of Western countries that had offered to accept refugees from Kosovo. His relatives from Kacanik are now scattered from Norway to England to Australia, a world away from both Kacanik and his new home outside Atlanta.

Qendrim was not quite six years old when his family arrived in Georgia. Now twelve and a half, he still remembered his first day of school, at McClendon Elementary. He knew no English, and none of the other kids.

"I was scared," Qendrim said. "I didn't know what to do. I didn't know where to go."

Qendrim's first friends were other Albanian and Bosnian Muslim kids he met in his apartment complex. As he learned English, he made friends at school. Xhalal took his son to the kids' soccer program at the Clarkston Community Center, where Qendrim met Luma and joined her refugee soccer team. The Fugees had since become the center of Qendrim's social life. He had grown close with Eldin, the Bosnian goalie, who lived in the same apartment complex. Qendrim and Eldin had their own morning ritual. On weekdays, their parents left their apartments soon after dawn for their long commutes to work. Qendrim would get dressed and walk down the driveway of the complex to Eldin's, where they would play video games or watch ESPN until it was time to go outside and wait for the school bus. They were best friends. Qendrim had become close with his other teammates as well: Grace, the midfielder from the Congo, who lived up the street; Josiah and Jeremiah, the Liberians; Bienvenue, the Burundian; Shahir, who was from Afghanistan; Robin and Idwar Dikori, the Sudanese brothers. Having friends from all over the world seemed perfectly normal to Qendrim; it was all he had known since arriving in the United States. Qendrim was smaller than most of his teammates, but he had their respect; when he called out directions during games, the others listened. Qendrim had come to feel that the other players were more than just teammates.

"It's like they're all from my own country," he said. "They're my brothers."

While the Under Fifteens were struggling to keep their team together, Qendrim and the Under Thirteens were beginning to gel. They had started the season with a tie and a loss but had since won their last two games, putting them in a position to actually win their division. Their play was improving, they were communicating better and with more confidence, and above all, they were having fun.

During practice, the players would strike out on their laps

at their own pace; Qendrim, Josiah, Jeremiah, Bien, and the Dikoris would take off, while Eldin, Mafoday, and Santino—the recently arrived Sudanese refugee—would follow, each at his own, slower pace. On Wednesday, though, as Luma was watching her Under Seventeen team scrimmage, she looked over to see the Thirteens running together in a kind of chorus line: the faster players had slowed down for the slower players, who in turn had sped up so as not to hold their teammates back. They ran like this for fifteen minutes or so, at which point the boys began to clap in rhythm with their strides. Eventually the boys began to chant.

"Who are the kings?" someone would shout to the group.

"The Fugees!" the team would answer.

Luma stayed focused on the older boys' scrimmage, but the Thirteens wouldn't be ignored. They chanted louder with each pass until Luma finally turned around to see what the fuss was all about. When the Thirteens saw they had their coach's attention, someone else called out: "Who is the queen?"

"Luma!" the boys shouted.

When Luma shook her head in confusion, the boys tumbled to the ground, laughing. It was a small, silly moment, but it also showed that boys from thirteen different countries and a wide array of ethnicities and religions and who spoke different languages were creating their own inside jokes. Even Mohammed Mohammed, the Iraqi Kurd whose family had arrived in the United States only a few months before the season and who spoke almost no English at all, was chanting at the top of his lungs and laughing as if someone had just told him the funniest joke he'd ever heard.

*   *   *

As the boys became more comfortable with one another, Luma was getting a better feel for her roster and for the ways she could move players around for different effects. She had learned, for example, that Bien was a kind of secret weapon. She would keep him hidden on defense for the first half or so of a game, then switch him to offense as the other team tired. By the time the competition realized the threat—usually when Bien fired a perfect cross or let loose with a bicycle kick—it was often too late to react.

Jeremiah could play both offense and defense equally well, just as he could kick the ball equally well with his left and his right foot, making him a threat on corner kicks from either side. Mohammed Mohammed was proving a tough defender despite his pint size. On offense, the Fugees' strength was at left forward in Josiah, whose runs down the sideline had resulted in a half-dozen goals so far. Qendrim was a good midfielder, great at directing his teammates, while Shahir, a quiet left midfielder, was getting more confident with each practice.

There was still a weakness on the Under Thirteens, though, in goal: Eldin and Mafoday, the heavyset young man from Gambia with the blinding smile. A good goalie was quick and determined. Ideally, attacking players should fear the keeper, especially when they took the ball in to the goalie box. Eldin and Mafoday inspired no fear. Standing in goal with their innocent, goofy smiles, they seemed less likely to take out an attacking forward than to hug him and invite him over to play. But Eldin and Mafoday had been with the team since the beginning. They were on time. They did their homework. So Luma had resolved to coach around their weaknesses.

20

Showdown at Blue Springs

"**C**oach," Mafoday said in a whisper, *"it's all white people."*
The Under Thirteens were walking onto the home field of the Blue Springs Liberty Fire in Loganville, Georgia, an old southern town down the road from other old southern towns with names such as Split Silk and Between. Luma looked around. It was true. Loganville was more than 90 percent white, and there wasn't so much as a suntan on the faces of the Liberty Fire or their parents. Luma reminded Mafoday that the Fugees rarely faced teams with black players.

"I know," Mafoday said. "But they are *all* white."

"Let it go," Luma said.

The Blue Springs Liberty Fire had a 3–2 record, but they were capable of scoring a lot of goals. Three weeks before, they had beaten one team 10–0. The Fugees were groggy.

The game was at nine a.m. Luma had called her players the night before to remind them of the early start. It was chilly out, so she wouldn't have them walking to the library for pickup, as was the custom. Instead, the bus would go from complex to complex to pick the players up. She expected everyone to be waiting and ready. One by one the sleepy Fugees had climbed onto the bus—all except for Jeremiah. He wasn't waiting out front, and there was no sign of life at the Ziatys' apartment. Luma knew that Beatrice had been working a night shift at the box factory. She would be sound asleep. So Luma told Tracy to knock on the door. Startled awake, Jeremiah grabbed his uniform and dashed to the bus. At game time, he was more or less sleepwalking.

Blue Springs struck first, taking the lead on an easy shot from ten yards out. The Fugees were still not fully awake. They were getting knocked around. Grace caught a hand to the face and crumpled over in pain. Qendrim was bounced like a pinball between the bigger Blue Springs midfielders. He was already frustrated.

"You better watch out," Qendrim said at one point to a Blue Springs player who'd gotten away with a push.

"What are you going to do about it?" the boy asked.

Qendrim didn't have a comeback for that one—he was too small to do much harm to anyone, and he knew that if he tried anything rough, Luma would bench him. So he sucked it up. A few minutes later, Qendrim was chasing after a free ball in the Blue Springs goal box when the goalie took him out at the knees. Play was stopped, and Qendrim was taken to the sideline wincing in pain.

With her team trailing 1–0 at halftime, Luma lit into

them. They were playing lazy soccer, she said. They were dribbling too much and not looking for the open man. And they were allowing themselves to get pushed around. Luma made just one adjustment, moving Jeremiah from defense up to midfield, where he could potentially set up Josiah. Qendrim's knee was still throbbing, but channeling the toughness he'd learned from his professional-soccer-playing grandfather, Qendrim told Luma he was ready to go back in.

"When I'm hurt and, like, we have to win because it's a hard team," he boasted later, "I just take the pain."

Just two minutes into the second half, Josiah made his way through three defenders, dribbling the whole way, before finding himself with a clear shot. He wheeled in behind the Blue Springs defenders and blasted a clean shot from fifteen yards out: 1–1. The Fugees were awake.

A few minutes later, Blue Springs was attacking when Mohammed Mohammed went in for a tackle from behind. He missed the ball and took out the Blue Springs forward—a nasty foul. The referee blew the whistle, and Blue Springs quickly set up for a direct kick from nearly twenty-five yards out. The ball sailed over the Fugees' wall, across the face of the goal and just into the top far corner. It was an amazing shot, and Eldin didn't stand a chance. It was 2–1, Blue Springs.

Luma decided it was time to deploy her secret weapon. Quietly, she signaled to Bien to swap with Jeremiah from defense to center midfielder. The boys switched positions, and to Luma's relief, the Blue Springs coach didn't seem to notice. Moments later, the Fugees managed a long pass down the field. Bien controlled the ball, and tapped a pass to a streaking

Idwar Dikori, who got the ball into the net. As he did, the linesman raised his flag: offside. The goal didn't count.

The Fugees, though, weren't upset. There would be other chances. Minutes later, Qendrim and Bien worked the ball toward the goal. Qendrim controlled a pass at the top of the box, and crossed it to Bien. For a moment, as the Blue Springs defenders converged, Bien looked as though he would pass it back to Qendrim, who was now unmarked. But Bien fired a shot instead, surprising everyone, including the Blue Springs keeper. It was a goal; the game was now tied again, at 2–2.

"Mark number three!" came a voice from the Blue Springs sideline, calling out Bien's number. "She just changed him!"

Shhh! thought Luma.

The next few minutes were frantic. Both teams were playing hard, and the close game had drawn the attention of parents and players on other local teams scheduled for games later in the morning. Blue Springs defenders now covered Bien, who was being set upon each time he touched the ball. But with five minutes left in the game, Bien again found himself on the receiving end of a pass. He looked upfield. Out of the corner of his eye, Bien spotted an orange jersey in open space: Idwar. Bien paused, then flicked a pass to Idwar, who volleyed it into the net. With minutes to go, the Fugees were finally ahead, 3–2.

Blue Springs wasn't finished. They sent a long pass down the field, and a Blue Springs forward managed to slip behind the Fugees defense. The ball was the only thing between him and Eldin in the Fugees' goal. The forward sprinted downfield; he'd have a shot. Out of the corner of her eye, Luma caught a glimpse of a streaking orange jersey: it was her youngest player, Robin Dikori, whose older brother, Idwar, had just scored. Tiny Robin slipped between the Blue Springs player and the ball, and kicked it clear.

Where did he come from? Luma wondered.

A moment later, the referee blew the whistle to signal the end of the game. Luma was thrilled. Her team hadn't given up, had played as a unit, and had come from behind—a sign of toughness and resolve. And the victory put the Under Thirteen Fugees within striking distance of first place, if they could keep winning. The boys were excited too. They broke into song and began dancing as a group, to the surprise of their hosts.

As the Fugees walked off the field toward their bus, a man on the Blue Springs sideline called out to them.

"I'd have paid money to watch that game!" he said.

21

Coming Apart

A day later, on Sunday, it was the Under Fifteens' turn for a big away game, against a Roswell Soccer Club team called the Santos, from an affluent suburb north of Atlanta. The Santos, contenders for the division championship, were well coached, disciplined, and quick. The Under Fifteen Fugees were still very much a work in progress. After their big win in their first game back after Luma's enforced hiatus, the Fifteens had lost 4–1 to a middle-of-the-pack team. Tito's shooting, the canceled practices that followed, and the change of practice venues had prevented the new team from getting into anything like a groove. Also, Mandela's mood had gotten worse. He missed his old Liberian teammates, and he seemed less committed to the Fugees.

After the starting whistle, it was the Fugees who

threatened first. Mandela bolted through the Santos defense and made a dash for the goal. The Santos goalie stepped forward to cut off his attack. Mandela tapped the ball out to Muamer, the new Bosnian forward. Only Muamer wasn't there to receive the pass, and the ball rolled out of bounds. Mandela barked at Muamer in frustration. His teammates glanced at one another. Mandela, it was clear, was in one of his moods.

A few minutes later, Kanue was shoved in the back while going for a ball in the Fugees' box. But the referee blamed Kanue himself for the confusion of flying bodies. It was a foul in the box, and a penalty shot for the Santos.

"Kanue—stop it!" Mandela yelled from midfield.

The Santos converted on the penalty kick to take a 1–0 lead. Minutes afterward, a Santos striker snuck behind Kanue, Alex, and Hamdu on defense and fired off a shot. Ervin, the Fifteens' goalie, dove to the right. The ball sailed past his fingertips and into the net. As the Santos were celebrating, Mandela laid into Ervin.

A few minutes after that score, the same forward for Roswell snuck behind the Fugees defense and blasted another shot past Ervin. It was now 3–0. Again, Mandela laid into the goalie. Ervin shrugged and shook his head: he wasn't getting any help on defense, he said. For the rest of the half, whenever he got the ball, Mandela turned and made a lonely dash for the Santos' goal, refusing to pass to his open teammates.

The runs all failed; Mandela lost control of the ball once, and twice it was stolen by Santos defenders. When the referee blew the whistle at halftime, the Fugees trailed 3–0. Luma was angry, but she remained calm. She ordered

Mandela to sit on the bench and told the rest of her players to follow her to midfield and to take a knee. They were bunching up in the middle on offense, she said. Muamer was dribbling too much and not keeping his head up to look for open teammates. Sampson, a Liberian who sometimes played goalie, she said, would move to center mid—Mandela's position.

"Thank you," several players said, grateful to hear that Mandela wouldn't come back into the game.

Mandela was sitting alone now, out of hearing range. He grabbed the bib of his sweat-soaked jersey, pulled it up over his face, and stretched it over his head, to block out the sun, the game, everything.

The Fugees played better soccer in the second half, even with one of their most talented players sitting on the bench. They spread the ball around and managed to score. But the Santos were in better shape and had been together for years. They were great on offense, and added one goal, and another, and another. When Luma gathered her players at the end of the game, the score was 6–1.

"What they got you on was you're way out of shape," she told them. "You made some sloppy mistakes on defense, and you weren't aggressive enough. So we have a lot of stuff to work on this week. You show up promptly at five to start— not to change, not to complain about how much running you're going to do. You show up at five to start practicing. All right? We've got a lot of work to do."

Luma led her players toward the parking lot and the team bus. She ordered Natnael and Mandela into her Volkswagen. They set off on a long, silent ride back to Clarkston.

*   *   *

"I've got this problem," Luma said to Natnael. "I need your advice. I've got this kid who shows up to practice when he feels like it. He cusses at his teammates. He disrespects his teammates. He won't even talk to his coach at practice. The only time he'll talk to his coach is when he needs something. He'll only do it over the phone."

Mandela squirmed but said nothing.

Luma told Natnael of the things she'd done for this player: When his free lunches at school were cut off because his mother hadn't properly filled out the paperwork, Luma took care of it. When his family was hungry, Luma had taken them food. When they needed help moving, Luma helped them move.

"The problem is, I just love his mom and his brother so much that I think I'm willing to let some things go," Luma said. "And I think I shouldn't have. Because I wouldn't have let them go for anyone else."

Mandela's eyes were fixed straight ahead.

"And so," Luma continued, "what am I supposed to do?"

Natnael watched the passing cars through the window. He said nothing.

"Natnael," Luma pressed. "What would *you* do, if you were the coach?"

Mandela was Natnael's friend. They had played together for two years, and they had worked to make sure the Under Fifteens could continue, against the odds. Natnael knew what it felt like to be a young man caught between worlds. He knew Mandela had been separated from the few Liberian friends he had who understood exactly what he was going through. Natnael also knew how frustration could turn into rage. He dealt with it himself. At the same time, Natnael had found a way to contain his anger and to find a place for himself on the team he, Mandela, and Kanue had worked to preserve. He knew it was possible. He took no pleasure in it, but Natnael knew the answer to Luma's question.

"Let him go," he said.

A few minutes later, Luma pulled her Volkswagen into the apartment complex off Indian Creek Way where the Ziatys lived. Luma's first words to Mandela came when they pulled into a parking space in front of his family's front door.

"For a while I expected you to be like Jeremiah," she told him. "Actually, you're a better athlete—but you don't have the discipline or the respect to play. You don't respect me, and you don't respect your team."

Mandela's expression remained blank. He didn't respond.

"Get out," Luma told him. "Don't call me Coach, and don't ever call me again."

Luma spent the evening and most of the next day in her apartment. She didn't want to talk to anyone. She didn't want to be around the kids for fear that she might say something she would later regret. So she kept to herself.

"It's like a kid you were hoping . . . and a family you're really close to . . . ," she said, trying to explain before interrupting herself.

"You don't want to give up," she said.

22

Hanging On at Home

The first full-time job for many refugees in Clarkston was cleaning and butchering just-killed chickens at local chicken processing plants. Many such plants around Atlanta ran twenty-four hours a day, and many refugees, starting out at the bottom, ended up taking jobs on the night shift. Managers didn't care what language workers spoke, as long as they showed up on time. And anyway, it was too loud in a chicken plant to carry on a conversation.

With a newborn baby girl to take care of and no husband around, Generose—the mother of Alex, Bien, Ive, and six-month-old Alyah—needed income, but she couldn't take just any job. She spoke almost no English and couldn't afford day care for Alyah. There was one obvious option: a night-shift job at a chicken processing plant.

The plants were always looking for new workers, so Generose had no problem finding a plant with an opening. Her shift ran from late afternoon to two in the morning; with the commute, she would get home just after three a.m., in time for a few hours of sleep before the boys woke up for school. The idea of leaving one's family at home and driving an hour to work at a factory to get paid by the hour struck Generose as a weird quirk of American society. Far worse than the actual work was the idea of being so far away from her children. Her boys—fifteen, thirteen, and seven—were at home alone with an infant.

Taking care of Alyah in the evenings fell mostly to Alex, the quiet defender for the Under Fifteen Fugees, who would hurry home after soccer practice in time for Generose to leave for work. He fed Alyah in the early evening, warming milk in the microwave and stirring in powdered baby food, which he would then spoon into her mouth as he held her on his lap. After Alyah was fed, Alex would turn his efforts to making dinner for his brothers while Bien and Ive watched television or did their homework. After dinner, Alex cleaned the kitchen, scrubbing the pans and wiping down the counters and stove top with the same graying cotton rag.

Alyah was a beautiful child with long, thin fingers and perfectly formed little lips. She rarely cried. She could sit for an hour or more in her walker without so much as a peep, gazing calmly at her brothers or at guests with her giant brown eyes. Alyah seemed to understand that she was loved and safe. After all, she had a team taking care of her. She spent much of the day sleeping in a *kanga* on her mother's back as Generose worked in the apartment, cleaning or cooking. In the evenings, when the boys came home, they would pick up Alyah and carry her around like a rag doll. Alyah seemed content to bop along for the ride, and if she was accidentally dropped onto the carpet, say, by seven-year-old Ive, she was less likely to cry than to look up at him with a quiet frown: another little sister convinced her big brother was a klutz.

One evening after practice, Alex came home weary and set about making dinner. He put some hot dogs in a pan for himself and his brothers and placed it on the stove. Then he got to work on Alyah's dinner. He washed a plastic container in the sink, poured in a dollop of milk, and placed the container in the microwave. Alyah was hungry now, and as she sat in her walker in the next room, she was crying out for food. Bien was on the sofa doing his homework, while Ive was lost in an episode of *The Simpsons*. Alyah's cry rose to a shriek as Alex waited for the microwave to beep. He stirred in the formula and tested the steaming mixture with his finger. It was too hot. He stirred some more and blew into the container to cool the food. The hot dogs were sizzling in the skillet. Alex then hurried into the living room to Alyah, who was still crying. Bien had put down his book and was bouncing his little sister on his knee, but she was in no mood to play. Alex took over. He perched Alyah on his knee, leaned her back into the crook where his arm met his body, and began to feed her, blowing on each spoonful until it was cool. Alyah was happy. She ate sloppily. With the small spoon, Alex patiently scraped the dripping food from Alyah's chin and the corners of her lips. Alyah's eyes lit up with each slurp of her dinner.

The smoke came first as a faraway scent, and then as a thundercloud rolling from the kitchen into the living room: the hot dogs. Alex put the food down, propped Alyah against the arm of the sofa, and ran into the kitchen. The hot dogs had melted into a black goo in the skillet, which was now billowing a foul-smelling smoke. Alex grabbed the wet rag he used to clean the kitchen, took the scalding skillet by the handle, and hurried to the sliding door at the back of the kitchen. He dropped the pan on the small back porch, then closed the door to keep the smoke out. By now Bien and Ive had appeared at the kitchen door. Alyah was crying in the other room.

The three boys stood quietly and watched the skillet smoke through the glass.

"What was that?" Ive asked finally.

"Dinner," Bien said.

When Mandela Ziaty walked into his apartment after getting kicked off the Fugees, he walked past his mother, Beatrice, without saying a word and went upstairs to his room. Beatrice asked him what was wrong, but he wouldn't answer. It took another few days for Beatrice to learn what had happened, which came when Mandela announced he wouldn't be going to practice.

"Why you can't go to practice?" Beatrice asked him.

"Mandela quit from the team," Jeremiah told her.

"Jeremiah, shut up your mouth," Mandela said.

Beatrice was worried for Mandela. Without soccer, he would be free in the afternoons and evenings to roam around Clarkston, to get into trouble. She'd been mugged herself there. Tito had been shot right in front of their apartment complex. Beatrice worked a night shift, folding cardboard at a packaging factory that made boxes for takeout pizza chains. While she was at work, Mandela would be free to do as he pleased.

"He ain't got nothing to do," Beatrice said.

A few days later, Beatrice overheard Mandela talking to his younger brother. "Jeremiah, I want to talk to Coach," Mandela said.

"Why you want to talk to Coach?" Jeremiah asked him.

"Why you want to talk to her?" Beatrice asked her son.

"I just want to talk to her," Mandela said. He didn't appreciate all the questioning, Beatrice could tell, so she let up. But in Mandela's room, there was a sign that perhaps he missed the Fugees more than he was saying. His bed was a mattress on the floor. The walls were bare but for one item. On the wall over his pillow, Mandela had carefully hung a pair of light blue shorts and a jersey of the same color: his old Fugees uniform.

23

The Dikoris

After her falling-out with Mandela, Luma tried to regroup. Between coaching and helping the families of players and employees, she had had little time for rest or for dealing with the details of her own life. Phone calls and emails were going unanswered. A brake light had burned out on her Volkswagen, and she had been too busy to replace it. And every time it seemed as though Luma might get a break, another team-related crisis would surface.

On the soccer field, though, things were looking up. The move to Milam Park had invigorated the Fugees, and having a proper field allowed Luma to work on her teams' weaknesses.

This coming weekend, the Under Thirteens would be put to the test. On Saturday, October 21, they were set to face their toughest competition of the season—the Athens United Gold Valiants, a team that was undefeated. The game was in Athens, a good hour and a half from Clarkston. Luma believed the Thirteens had a chance. They were communicating better with one another. Luma herself had a better feel for the roster and how to rotate players through positions to create opportunities. And the team had discovered a secret weapon of sorts: the Dikori brothers.

Idwar and Robin Dikori were playing their first season with the Fugees and were among the team's youngest players. Idwar was twelve, Robin just nine. Robin was small, with tiny cat feet and legs that seemed to extend to his armpits. Idwar was taller, with a thin frame. With their wiry builds, the boys didn't look threatening. They were quiet, shy, and seemingly unassertive. But over the previous few games, the Dikoris had each displayed speed that made the rest of the players look as though they were running in slow motion. Luma knew they were quick, but her eyes were opened to the boys' potential at that moment in the Blue Springs game when Robin had appeared out of nowhere to clear the ball. If she could find a way to use the boys' quickness against Athens, Luma felt the Fugees had a chance to knock off the best team in the league.

The Dikoris were from the Nuba Mountains of central Sudan, an area the size of South Carolina, with more than a million people. The land is divided between bare mountain slopes and fertile valleys that support both grazing and farming. The Nuba region existed between African culture in the south and Arab culture in the north, prompting Yousif Kuwa, the late rebel leader of the Nuba, to declare his people "prisoners of geography." In the Nuba region, some fifty different ethnic groups, including Christians, Muslims, and practitioners of traditional African religions, lived in peace.

But the Islamist regime that came to power in Sudan in a 1989 coup wanted access to the vital soil of the Nuba valleys. During a dry season in 1991 and 1992, the government in Khartoum decided to drive the indigenous groups out. The government harassed civilians until they fled the fertile valleys—land the government began distributing to its cronies. The campaign was brutal. Bombs were dropped on the clusters of round straw huts that made up villages in the Nuba. Convoys of government troops terrorized locals with random killings and a campaign of rape intended to move the villagers to so-called peace camps. A 1998 report by the U.S. Committee for Refugees estimated that approximately two hundred thousand people, or slightly less than a fifth of the total population of the Nuba region, were killed in what it called the Nuba genocide.

Robin and Idwar's parents, Daldoum and Smira Dikori, were relatively well off before this campaign of violence began. They lived in a fertile valley, the kind the government in Khartoum craved. Daldoum had a high school education. He had land to farm, and livestock. The Dikoris were members of the Moro tribe, a mostly Christian group numbering close to one hundred thousand, and among the largest ethnic groups in the Nuba. Their eldest son, Shamsoun, a quiet young man with ink-black skin and bright eyes, said that the many ethnic groups in the area got along well when the family lived there, and he remembers how it was all explained to him as a child.

"We say that there are ninety-nine different mountains in Nuba and each has its own tribe," he said.

Robin and Idwar were too young to remember the violence that came raining down on the family's village in the form of fire and metal. But Shamsoun, now seventeen and a member of the Under Seventeen Fugees, remembers the first time he saw the planes.

"We were playing outside and we thought it was birds," he said. "Then the bombs started to fall and everyone started running."

When the bombings started, villagers fled for the mountains, as the government had hoped. The men, Shamsoun said, first escorted their children and wives into the hills—journeys that took days—and then returned to their villages to save what possessions they could before the government convoys arrived. Daldoum was lucky. He managed to round up a few goats and cows, and a donkey to help him carry goods and farm the land. The family built a hut in a small makeshift village with other Moro, avoiding the "peace camps" and farming the surrounding hillsides to produce enough food to survive. After five months of growing barely enough to feed itself, the family gave up and went to stay with relatives who had moved to Khartoum.

"They had open markets where you could buy stuff," Shamsoun remembers. "It was pretty hot. It was not like the Nuba Mountains. I didn't feel safe."

*   *   *

The Islamist government in Khartoum didn't make life easy for the Christians who moved to the capital looking for work, food, and housing. The government wanted to force military service on the men—and to send them back into the Nuba Mountains to continue the campaign of terror. Government-backed henchmen demanded that Christians convert to Islam and change their Christian names to Muslim ones. Eventually, the Dikori family decided to leave and to join the tens of thousands of Sudanese refugees streaming into Egypt. Daldoum put together enough money to transport his family from Khartoum to Egypt, a two-day journey on a packed and run-down train. The Dikoris made it to Cairo, where they connected with friends.

Cairo was no paradise. After a failed assassination attempt on the Egyptian president Hosni Mubarak in Addis Ababa that he blamed on the Sudanese government, entering Egypt for most Sudanese meant entering illegally. Refugees were not allowed to work, and they were not eligible for subsidized housing. Sudanese in Egypt also faced racial discrimination—they were disparaged as "chocolata" or "honga bonga" by some hostile Egyptians, who were growing weary of their uninvited guests.

Daldoum had no intention of keeping his family—his wife, Smira; daughters, Sara, Gimba, and Banga; and sons, Shamsoun, Idwar, and Robin—in such conditions for very long. He went to the crowded United Nations refugee office in Cairo and applied for resettlement. In 2000, the family received word that they had been accepted for relocation to the United States and a place called Georgia.

The Dikoris arrived in May 2000. Idwar was just six and

Robin four, but Shamsoun was eleven, and remembers well his reaction when he stepped off the plane. He was afraid, he said, of the escalators in the Atlanta airport, which looked like the teeth of some giant trash compactor. His father nudged him along, and young Shamsoun held on for dear life as the moving stairway carried him toward the unknown.

The family did their best to settle in. They were taken first to Jubilee Partners, where Tracy volunteered and helped refugee families adjust to their new lives. The Dikoris took English lessons and learned about American culture. The kids enrolled in school. Their English improved. Daldoum got a job at a construction supply company and saved enough for a car, a Mazda minivan that could accommodate his big family. And on November 27, 2002, Daldoum and Smira decided to take their children to visit a family of fellow Sudanese refugees, who, like the Dikoris, had made it safely to the United States and been resettled in Tennessee. The trip was also a chance to explore the family's new sense of personal liberty. In their new home, they were free to travel as they liked, without fear of getting stopped by authorities hostile toward their ethnicity or religion. The Wednesday before the family's second Thanksgiving in America, they piled into the Mazda van, all eight of them. Daldoum took the wheel proudly, and the family set off for Tennessee in the late afternoon.

The family made it to Tennessee, about two hours north of Atlanta, and was driving through the hills just north of the Georgia and Alabama state lines, and just east of Chattanooga. Daldoum was traveling in the left lane of the westbound side of Interstate 24 between mile markers 164 and 165, a gradual left-hand curve. A trucker named Thomas Combs was traveling ahead of the van, and looked in his side-view mirror just in time to see the vehicle drift to the left and onto the shoulder between the west- and eastbound arteries of the roadway. Daldoum jerked the wheel to the right. Combs saw the van swerve onto the interstate and begin to tip onto its left side. The van then rolled violently, flipping numerous times across both westbound lanes before coming to a stop, upside down, on the grassy shoulder. Combs hit the brakes, pulled off the road, and ran back to help.

Shamsoun Dikori came to lying prone on the ground beside the wreck. There was a woman looking down at him, trying to wake him up—he remembers her as a nurse who had stopped to help. His father appeared a moment later, looking down at him, asking if Shamsoun was all right.

"I could see from his face that something was really wrong," Shamsoun said. Robin, Idwar, and Shamsoun were taken to two separate hospitals. The younger boys had only cuts and bruises, but Shamsoun had a head injury that required surgery and a weeklong hospital stay. Soon the boys were back near Atlanta, a world away from where they'd grown up, and now without their mother and three sisters, who had died in the crash.

The next months were trying. Robin began to act out at school, while Idwar retreated into silence. Daldoum continued to work, but he could offer little comfort to his children.

"Our father doesn't show a lot of affection—that's how it is with African parents," Shamsoun said. "Robin started messing up in school—not paying attention, getting mad quicker. Idwar keeps most things to himself and didn't talk to anyone else about problems he was having.

"It's hard to live without your mom," he said.

As the oldest, Shamsoun did his best to support his younger brothers. But he was a teenager himself, grieving and lost in a strange world. He took comfort in the occasional pickup games of soccer that he played on weekends and after school. But the games were for older boys and men; Idwar and Robin were too young to join in. During one of those neighborhood games at Indian Creek Elementary, Shamsoun looked at the other end of the field and saw a group of young refugees trying out for the Fugees. He asked a friend for an introduction to the coach and joined in, bringing his brothers later on. They were young—Robin especially, who was four years behind most of the players on Luma's youngest team. But she brought Idwar and Robin on board, assuming they'd find roles on the team as they got older. That was before she recognized how fast they were.

Robin calmed down at school and became outgoing with his teammates. Idwar, still quiet and shy, became a confident young man on the field. Soccer, Shamsoun said, kept the boys sane.

"It kept our minds from thinking about what happened," he said. "We made friends—kids from different cultures. It broadened our minds, and we weren't the only ones going through hard times. That's why the team is so close. It became our family."

24

"What Are You Doing Here?"

On the morning of October 21, the Under Thirteen Fugees piled into the white YMCA bus in the parking lot of the Clarkston Public Library and set out for Athens to take on the Athens United Gold Valiants. It was a one-and-a-half-hour drive, so the boys settled in. Tracy drove the bus while Luma led the way in her yellow Volkswagen. The drive took them out of the bustle of Atlanta and through small towns in the Georgia countryside. Luma cued up her iPod, which was plugged into her car stereo, and turned up the music. For the first time in a long while, she was able to daydream.

Near Monroe, Georgia, about an hour east of Atlanta, Luma was cruising in the right-hand lane when she looked out the driver's-side window and saw a Georgia state police car riding alongside her. Luma looked at her speedometer. She wasn't speeding. A moment later, the trooper eased his cruiser behind Luma's Volkswagen and turned on his flashing lights.

The brake light, Luma thought.

The light had been on a long list of personal errands Luma had put off to deal with her team and her players' families. She eased onto the shoulder and began to slow, with the trooper behind her. The bus carrying the team continued on. Luma looked at her watch; if this didn't take too long, she could still get to Athens in time for a full warm-up.

The officer approached and asked for Luma's license, then disappeared for a moment into his car. By now, the kids on the bus were getting agitated. Some of the boys had seen Luma get pulled over through the rear window of the bus. They asked Tracy what was happening. She wasn't certain but reassured them that Luma would be on her way shortly. Meanwhile, the officer approached Luma's car again. Her license had been suspended, he informed her, and ordered her out of the car.

Luma was puzzled. There was no reason her license should have been suspended. She'd been ticketed only once in recent memory, for an expired registration, and she had paid the fine on time. The trooper had no way of looking into that on a weekend. He only knew what the computer told him. Under Georgia law, he said, he had to arrest her. The trooper ordered Luma to turn around and put her hands behind her back. She did, and a moment later felt the cold steel of the officer's handcuffs on her wrists.

By now, Tracy had turned the bus around and was pulling onto the shoulder behind the cop's cruiser.

Luma asked that she be allowed to give the team's player cards to the bus driver so the team could go ahead to the game without her, and pleaded with the officer to remove the handcuffs while they were in front of the kids.

"If you promise not to hit me," he said—a joke.

Luma didn't laugh.

The officer obliged. Luma took the player cards to Tracy—the referee would need them to verify the identities and ages of the players. Then she addressed her players. She told them she wouldn't be able to make their game. She told them they knew what to do. She expected them to win without her. Luma had hoped to reassure the Fugees, but her voice was shaking.

The Fugees sat uneasily on the bus. Several had seen or heard of family members getting carted off—or worse—by police for the pettiest of offenses. Santino Jerke's uncle had been shot and killed in front of him by uniformed Sudanese government soldiers for stealing a chicken. Shahir Anwar's family had been hounded by Taliban soldiers because his mother ran a school for girls. The boys' coach and guide through the unfamiliar world where their families had settled was getting hauled off by the police. Some of the boys began to cry.

Josiah Saydee, the Liberian forward and team leader, was sitting in the last row. As the bus pulled back onto the highway, he turned around and looked through the rear window to see Luma getting into the backseat of the police cruiser. In hushed tones, Josiah told his teammates sitting near him what he had seen: Coach Luma was in a police car. She was going to jail.

*   *   *

The Fugees unloaded from the team bus in the parking lot of the Athens United Soccer Club a little more than half an hour later. David Anderson, the Valiants' coach, saw their faces and got excited. The Valiants had been beating their opponents badly, and Anderson wanted a challenge. Anderson knew next to nothing about the Fugees when they showed up, but at a glance, he assumed they were a notch above the typical local team.

"You see certain nationalities," said Anderson, "and you say, 'These kids can play.'" But he also noted one important absence.

Where's their coach? he wondered.

The Walton County jail was a dull structure surrounded by a tangle of razor wire that ran along a chain-link fence and glistened in the sunlight. Inside, the trooper who had arrested Luma was handing her over to the custody of the Walton County Sheriff's Department. A clerk asked her to state her name.

"Luma," she said.

"How do you spell that?" the clerk asked.

"Don't bother," the trooper said, sliding her driver's license to the clerk.

The clerk noticed Luma's middle initial—H—and asked what it stood for.

"Hassan," Luma said.

The clerk cast a knowing glance at the arresting officer.

"Hassan?" she said. "Where's that from?"

"Jordan," said Luma.

"It's Arab?" the clerk asked. "What are you doing here?"

Luma started to explain that she was on the way to a soccer game when she had been pulled over, but she was cut off.

"What are you doing *here*—in the United States?" she was asked.

Luma didn't respond. It was time to get fingerprinted. When she had registered with the Immigration and Naturalization Service upon filing her green card application, Luma had been fingerprinted; her fingers were placed on an ink pad and carefully rolled over the card beneath. The woman at the Walton County jail had a different approach; she grabbed Luma's hand, inked her fingertips, and then slammed her hand down on the counter. For the first time, Luma began to feel afraid. Her wallet and sweatshirt were taken from her—the bailiff told Luma she couldn't wear the sweatshirt in the jail because it might be contaminated with lice. Bail was set at $759.50, and Luma was escorted into a holding cell with a group of women who looked no happier to be there than she was.

By now, Dave Anderson had learned that the Fugees' coach had been held up en route to the game, and he was curious to see how the team would fare without help from the sideline. Tracy did her best to encourage the boys, but she was not a soccer coach. The boys divvied up their positions and took the field. Robin and Idwar Dikori were unaware of the challenge that awaited them. It took the Valiants less than three minutes to score their first goal. Two minutes later, they scored again. Anderson could tell something was amiss; he knew from what he'd seen in the warm-ups that the Fugees could play, and yet on the field they looked lost. They were arguing with one another and giving Eldin, the goalie, a hard time. A few minutes later, the Valiants scored their third goal. The first half was not yet halfway over. Anderson scanned the Fugees' half of the field. Their heads had begun to drop. It was a sign he'd come to know well from the Valiants' opponents.

Aw, man, Anderson thought. They're done.

The Valiants scored again. And again. At the half, they led 5–0.

When the Valiants came to the bench, Anderson told them he would be switching them up in the second half. The forwards would move to defense. The defenders would play offense. They understood why—the game was getting out of hand—but they were puzzled, unable to understand how a group of kids who seemed so talented in warm-ups could play so badly.

The Fugees spent halftime fighting over who would play where. Tiny Qendrim volunteered to replace Eldin at keeper, a move his teammates roundly rejected, even as they agreed a change was needed in the net. Half the team wanted Bien on defense, where he could clear the ball with his powerful kick; the other half wanted him at forward. Jeremiah would anchor the middle. Mafoday, usually the weaker of the two keepers, would take Eldin's place in the net. As the second half began, Anderson watched to see how the Fugees would respond. A few minutes in, he noticed something: their chins were up. They were going after the ball. The Valiants managed to blast a shot low and to the left. Heavyset Mafoday, whose vertical jump was perhaps three inches, dove and made the stop. A moment later, Jeremiah chased down a free ball and, attempting to clear it, blasted it into a Valiants' midsection with unexpected force. The player collapsed on the ground in pain and had to come out of the game. The Fugees hadn't caved. Midway through the second half, the score was still 5–0 when the Fugees were called for a foul in the box for slide tackling from behind. The Valiants would have a penalty shot.

Mafoday took his place in goal. With his stubby legs and broad waist supporting a big barrel chest, Mafoday appeared more like a fixture in goal than a potentially mobile obstacle. He looked vulnerable and almost lonely. Mafoday shook out his arms, put his hands on his knees, and stared into the narrowing eyes of the Valiants sharpshooter in shiny black and gold before him. The Valiants parents cheered the shooter on, while the Fugees players encouraged Mafoday with less confidence: there wasn't much difference, after all, between a five- and a six-goal lead.

The Valiants shooter surveyed the open net in front of him. He stepped toward the ball, flung his leg forward, and connected, firing a low, fast shot to the goalie's right. Mafoday Jawneh had made his decision. As the Valiants player made contact with the ball, Mafoday tipped to his right and began to fall. He extended his arms over his head and landed on the ground, stretched out and parallel with the crossbar. There was a thud, then a moment's pause as Mafoday and his teammates realized the ball had stopped in his gray padded goalie gloves—and stayed there, just in front of the end line: a save. The Fugees erupted in cheers and surrounded Mafoday.

A few minutes later, the referee blew the whistle three times: the final score was 5–0, Valiants. The Fugees hadn't given up a goal in the second half. They'd fought and held their own.

Sitting in the Walton County jail, Luma had lost all track of time. Eventually, her thoughts turned to Amman, her family, and especially her late grandmother, who had always told her as a child that things happened for a reason. What was the reason for this? Luma wondered. Was it a warning that she should change her middle name in America so she wasn't harassed? That she should pay more attention to her own life by making sure she took care of things like burned-out brake lights?

Luma heard her name being called. She stepped into a room with a view of the clerk's counter, where she saw Tracy signing papers and sliding them back to the clerk, then handing over cash for bail—$759.50 in exact change. A moment later, a door opened and Luma was free to go. She walked out of the building and directly onto the team bus, parked just in front of the Walton County jail.

Luma asked about the score and got the bad news: the Fugees had lost 5–0.

"This was my fault, and I had no excuse for not being there," she told her players. "I should have been there and I wasn't, and the way it happened probably messed you guys up."

"Mafoday stopped a penalty kick!" someone said.

"It was a really hard team, Coach," said Idwar Dikori.

"Were they better than you?" Luma asked.

"No!" the Fugees shouted in response.

"Come on, guys—were they?"

"No, Coach," said Robin, Idwar's little brother. "If you were there, we were going to beat them."

Back in Clarkston that night, Luma got a call from the nine-year-old brother of Grace Balegamire, a midfielder for the Under Thirteens. The boy's mother had gone to the hospital with his older brother and little sister, to visit a friend who had just had a baby. The boy was at home with his twin brother and Grace, but he was unhappy.

"I'm sad," he told Luma.

"Why are you sad?" she asked.

"I'm scared to be alone," he said.

"Oh, quit it," Luma said.

Luma hung up the phone and decided she had an errand to run.

She drove to the grocery store and picked up some sweet rolls, then headed over to the boy's apartment. When she arrived, he was in his bedroom with the door closed. Luma knocked, but the boy wouldn't answer. She coaxed him out eventually with the sweet rolls. The two sat and talked.

"I just had a bad day," he said.

Luma smiled. "Do you want to hear about a bad day?" she said.

"Yeah."

Luma told him everything. The cops, the jail, how she missed Grace's soccer game. He didn't buy any of it.

"Coach, don't lie," he said. "You would never go to jail."

"No, I went—ask Grace."

"If you were in jail, you wouldn't be here," he said.

"No—Tracy paid to get me out," Luma said.

"How much?"

"Enough for five hundred ice creams."

"If you pay five hundred ice creams you can come out of jail?" he asked.

Luma started to explain how bail worked, but then she caught herself, finally understanding the boy's confusion. The Balegamires' father was still locked up in Makala, the notorious central prison in Kinshasa. The government of the Democratic Republic of Congo had issued no word on when—or if—he would be released.

25

Halloween

On October 27, less than a week after Luma's arrest on the way to Athens, Reuters, the BBC, and the New York Times each published short notices about a prison riot in Kinshasa, the capital city of the Democratic Republic of Congo. The government reported that five inmates had been killed and that fourteen had escaped.

Joseph Balegamire, Paula's husband and the father of her children, was an inmate there. Paula called friends but could gather no information on her husband. So for now, she waited, hoping for a phone call to tell her whether Joseph was still an inmate, was among the dead, or, God willing, had escaped.

Halloween was not exactly a big holiday in Clarkston, Georgia. Many of the refugees had never heard of it. But after the arrest in Athens and the news at the Balegamires', Luma decided that the Fugees needed a break and an introduction to America's most sugary holiday. Luma arranged to use the YMCA's bus for the evening and called the parents of the Under Thirteen players to let them know that their sons would be home a bit later than usual. She stopped by a CVS and bought costumes—matching ninja outfits that were more or less black plastic sheets with hoods. She held a casual practice in which she scrimmaged and laughed with the kids, and then afterward surprised them all with the news that they were going trick-or-treating. The neighborhood Luma had in mind for the outing was not one any of the Fugees had seen before. It was a wealthy part of Decatur with a series of rolling narrow lanes that closed to traffic on Halloween each year to become a trick-or-treater's paradise. Nearly every house participated, and residents went all out: the adults wore costumes themselves and decorated their homes with spooky displays—witches and spiderwebs, ghosts and skeletons with flashing red lights for eyes—and had dungeon sound tracks blaring from upstairs windows. Behind each door there were staggering supplies of candy: giant boxes of Mars Bars, Hershey's Kisses, Snickers, Reese's Peanut Butter Cups, Jolly Ranchers, and huge, squirming nests of Gummi Worms.

As they bounced in the bus toward Decatur, Luma passed out the costumes, and the boys disappeared beneath their black plastic sheets, all except Mafoday. On top of his ninja robe, which stretched at the seams on his round frame, he wore a large pink feather boa and a rubber Elvis mask, odds and ends from the costume bin at the local pharmacy.

Luma handed out shopping bags for the candy they would

collect. It was the first Halloween for most of the Fugees, and they seemed unsure of what they were supposed to do, so Luma gave them instructions: ring doorbells, say "Trick or treat?" take a few pieces of candy, and say "Thank you."

The Fugees stood out in the neighborhood. They were the only trick-or-treaters to arrive by bus, and they were among the only children who weren't white. But the boys were too taken with the scene before them to notice. One by one they stepped off the bus and gazed at the wonderland they had entered.

Children in elaborate costumes roamed the streets by the hundreds. The cool evening air was filled with playful screams and laughter. There were no police to be seen, and no older boys standing around looking for trouble.

Luma told the boys that she and Tracy would stay behind to watch the bus. They were free to roam as they pleased. Halloween, to the Fugees, seemed almost too good to be true. Grace, Josiah, and Bien led the way to the first house, up a lighted walkway and a flight of brick steps. Nervously, Josiah rang the doorbell. A moment later, the door opened.

"My word!" a woman said, startled by the sight before her: a pack of small, dark-skinned faces and white eyes peering out from behind black plastic sheeting. The boys were scared silent by the reaction. Finally someone up front remembered the magic phrase: "Trick or treat!"

The woman passed a box full of candy through the doorway. One by one the Fugees dipped their hands in. The boys were careful, taking just one or two pieces. One by one they said thank you and moved aside for their teammates. The last in line was Mafoday, in his boa and Elvis mask, who waited patiently for his turn. When the other boys finally moved out of the way, he could scarcely believe his eyes: an entire box of candy for the taking. He plunged his two hands deep into the pile of shiny wrappers and took out a good pound of loot.

"Young man!" said the woman.

"Thank you!" Mafoday said, flashing his bright smile. He ran after his friends, his pink feather boa streaming behind him in the breeze.

The boys went through the neighborhood, venturing deep into culs-de-sac and up dark sidewalks to houses that many other kids avoided. If there was candy to be had, the Fugees were going to find it. The boys stuck together, and for the most part kept to themselves. Their only real interaction with American kids came about as a result of a misunderstanding. A group of American girls of fourteen or fifteen had dressed up as much younger girls—with pigtails and teddy bears, wearing pajamas and kiddie clothes. One was wearing a soccer uniform, shirt neatly tucked in, socks pulled up to her knees, like a peewee soccer player who had been carefully dressed by her mother. Grace Balegamire didn't understand that the getup was a costume and assumed instead that the girl had come straight from practice, as the Fugees had.

"What position do you play?" he asked her when they passed each other on the street.

"What position do you think I play?" the girl said sassily.

"You look like you play defense."

"Defense?" the girl said, now sounding every bit her age. "I think he just insulted me!"

With that, both the Fugees and the girls laughed, though no one seemed quite sure why, and went their separate ways.

*   *   *

A short while later, the Fugees headed back to the bus. Their plastic grocery sacks were bursting at the seams. A quiet fell over the boys. They were weary from all the walking, and crashing from their sugar highs. When they reached the bus, the boys picked through their stashes of candy and one by one paused to look up and take in the scene before them: the glimmering homes, the kids laughing and running freely around a neighborhood, the incredible costumes. Grace was asked what he thought of his first Halloween.

"Well," he said after careful consideration, "when you knock on somebody's door in Africa—they don't give you candy."

"Yep," Bien agreed, a bit wearily. "You'd be lucky if you got an egg."

Later that evening, after the bus had dropped the boys off at their apartments around Clarkston, Grace lay in bed, sleeping, when he was startled awake: gunshots—fired just below his second-story bedroom window. Grace knew better than to look outside, and instead stayed low in his room. He was afraid. A little while later, the police arrived. The sharp sound of their radios echoed in the parking lot and in the darkened stairwells of the apartment complex. A little while later, the cops pulled away. They'd made no arrests. Quiet returned. Grace closed his eyes and tried once again to sleep.

26

The Fifteens' Final Game

"**H**ow come you never told me your father was dead?" Natnael asked Joseph.

The two boys were friends—Natnael, the leader of the Under Fifteens, and Joseph, a veteran of the Under Seventeen Fugees—and were riding together in the backseat of a car on the way to the Fifteens' final game of the season. Joseph was coming along to give the younger team support.

"I don't really tell anybody," Joseph said, answering Natnael's question. "Because I don't want them asking all sorts of questions about it."

Natnael was curious now. He seemed startled that he didn't know such an important detail of his friend's life.

"Did you cry?" he asked Joseph.

"No," Joseph said. "I didn't cry."

Natnael considered the response.

"How can you not cry?" he asked finally.

"Well, if you don't know somebody—" Joseph cut himself off, and tried to think of an example.

"You got an uncle, right, in your old country?" he asked.

"No."

Joseph thought for another moment. He wanted to explain.

"Well, you got your mom, right?"

"Yeah," said Natnael.

"Well, if your mom died, you'd cry, right?"

"Yeah."

"But if you never knew your mom, then you wouldn't cry," Joseph said.

Natnael nodded. That was why his friend didn't cry at his father's death. He understood now.

A few minutes later, Natnael and the Under Fifteen Fugees took the field to warm up for their final game of the year. Joseph sat on the bench to cheer them on. It hadn't been the season Luma or the boys on the Fifteens had hoped. Their goal at the beginning of the fall had been to make the State Cup—a tournament for the area's best teams. Instead, they were fighting for their pride and against the threat of getting demoted to a lower division for next season.

The Fugees were in a playful mood, laughing and joking with one another, trying, it seemed, not to think too much about soccer. Two and a half months of stress had worn them out. Luma urged them to focus.

"You've got your last game of the season today—this is it,"

she told them beforehand. "The way you play today is going to tell me how you guys are going to play next year. Okay? So let's work it."

The Fugees were playing the Cobb YMCA Strikers. The Fugees had managed a win earlier in the season against a team that had beaten the Strikers. Today they stood a chance.

Despite Luma's efforts to wake them up, the Fugees played the early minutes in a daze. They were easily frustrated, and aside from Kanue—playing all out as usual—the players were walking and showing little intensity. The Strikers controlled the ball. They scored ten minutes into the half, and then again before the half, to lead 2–0. Luma was enraged: it was one thing to lose, and another thing not to try. *After all we've been through.*

"So, what's wrong?" she asked her players. "Is the ref cheating?"

"No," the boys said.

"Are they faster than you?"

"No."

"Are they better than you?"

"No," the boys said.

"So the score's two to nothing for what reason?"

Silence.

"I'll tell you why," Luma said, her voice rising. "Because you are a bunch of idiots. You do not know how to play soccer. You know how to play street ball. So everything that everyone has said about this team—that you don't deserve to play, that you don't know how to play as a team, because you don't have the discipline or the respect to play—it's true. Because you don't know how to play.

"If you want to play on the streets, let me know," Luma said finally. "Because this is a waste of my time."

Luma walked away from her players and the boys sat quietly for a moment, heads bowed. They were embarrassed by their play, wounded by their coach's comments, unsure what to do next.

"That's what I hate about her, man," one player said. "When she stops coaching us, then we're gonna lose *everything*."

"She's supposed to be mad, man," said Sebajden, the midfielder from Kosovo. "We're playing like little kids."

"Nobody get mad," said another boy.

"Let's make our coach happy, man," Sebajden said.

"We can do this. Come on."

The boys put their hands together a final time, chanted, "One, two, three—go Fugees!" and jogged back onto the field to try to save the afternoon.

They played harder, Kanue leading the way. Natnael scored on a long free kick. The Fugees attacked, and chased down free balls. But again the Fifteens made mistakes. They turned the ball over with sloppy throw-ins, and were called for offsides seemingly every time they managed to gain some momentum. Hamdu Muganga got called for a foul in the box, and the Strikers put away the penalty shot. The Fugees began to get frustrated, and to foul. When the referee blew his whistle, the score was 3–1, and the Under Fifteens' season was over.

The boys walked quietly toward Luma and sat down around her. Her tone had shifted. She was no longer angry or yelling, but she was every bit as serious as she had been at halftime.

"You knew better than I did, is why you lost," Luma told the boys afterward. "It's an embarrassment to sit on the sideline and see you do throw-ins with your feet up, and throw-ins with your feet stepping over the line. And it is an embarrassment to sit here as a coach and watch you miss open shots at goal. And it's even more of an embarrassment to see you lose your cool. That is not the team I coach.

"If you plan to continue with this team," Luma added, "it's my rules, my drills, my way."

Kanue and Natnael sat before her, their heads bowed. They had worked hard to keep their team together, and the season had fallen apart anyway. They'd have to find a way to win next year.

27

My Rules, My Way

Things were much different for the Under Thirteen Fugees. Though Luma was reluctant to admit it, her bond with the Thirteens was deeper than that with the older boys. She had been coaching some of them since her first season, when they were younger than ten years old. The Thirteens followed her system—my rules, my drills, my way—and their record, Luma felt, showed the results. After the Athens game, the Thirteens had tied two games and lost one, but they had never folded, and in each of the contests, they had fought until the very end. The Thirteens had clearly improved. They had learned their own strengths and kept their cool; they had received no red cards during the season. The boys looked out for one another. When Josiah heard that Santino, the quiet Sudanese boy who had arrived in the United States just

199

before the season, had no winter clothes, he dug around in a closet and found his old winter coat, which he gave to his teammate. No member of the Fugees, Josiah reasoned, should go cold.

The Under Thirteens played their final regular-season game on a dark, misty November afternoon in Lawrenceville, Georgia, against the Georgia Futbol Club. If they hoped to finish well, the Fugees needed to win and to avoid getting any red cards, which brought point deductions. They had to keep their cool. It wouldn't be easy. The team from Lawrenceville had managed some big wins earlier in the fall, defeating one club 10–0 and another 6–0, and they were bigger and taller than the Fugees.

Luma had a plan. The Fugees were to keep the ball on the ground, and whenever possible, to send the ball away from the middle and toward the wings, where Josiah and Idwar could use their speed and where the Fugees were less likely to get knocked around. If they got bumped, she told them, they were not to retaliate. Take the fouls, she told them, and above all, keep your cool.

"Let them push you down," Luma said. "I don't want anyone out there who's scared."

Before the game, the Fugees found themselves with some time to kill. A game between two older girls' teams was winding up on a nearby field. The boys were quickly drawn into the action—cheering at each shot and steal, laughing and trading high fives when one of the girls dribbled around a defender, leaving her competitor in the dust.

Soon it was time to take their positions on the field. But first Grace had an idea: he thought the Fugees should pray together. The idea presented a question; there were both Christians and Muslims on the team. How could they include everyone? With no help from Luma or any other adult, the boys quickly worked out a solution. Grace would offer a Christian prayer; Eldin, a Muslim one. The boys formed a circle at midfield, draped their arms around each other, and bowed their heads. Both Grace and Eldin felt more comfortable praying the way they'd been taught—in their native languages. No one objected as Grace prayed aloud in Swahili and Eldin in Bosnian, first for the health and safety of their teammates, and then, if God saw fit, for a victory.

"Amen," Grace said.

"Amen," the boys responded.

"Amin," said Eldin.

"Amin," said the boys.

Moments later, the game was under way. The Fugees attacked. Midway through the first half, Bien snuck through the Lawrenceville defense and dished a pass to Jeremiah, who quickly sent the ball across the field to Josiah. Josiah took a shot from twenty yards out: goal. The Fugees went ahead 1–0 and carried that lead into the half.

"One to nothing is not enough," Luma told the boys. "Keep calm. Keep your game. Start smiling. Let's start having a good time and let's kick some butt."

The Fugees started the half by attacking down the touchlines, as Luma had instructed them. Soon Jeremiah controlled a pass at the top right corner of the box, rolled around into the open space near the corner, and fired a shot clear across the middle that slipped between the goalie's fingers and the inside of the far post. The Fugees were up 2–0. A late foul in the box gave Lawrenceville a penalty shot to pull within a goal, but the Fugees held off the opposition to win the game 2–1.

The Fugees would finish third in their division, behind the Athens Gold Valiants and the Dacula Danger, a team the Fugees had tied 2–2 earlier in the season. As a reward for their hard work, Luma had registered the Fugees for the Tornado Cup, a tournament that would feature some of the best teams from around the state. The Under Thirteens had a week to prepare.

28

Tornado Cup

Luma knew that for the Under Thirteen Fugees to compete in the Tornado Cup, they needed an intense week of practice. Luma planned to put the Under Thirteens through three days of intense drills on crosses, corners, and free kicks, followed by a scrimmage on Thursday with the Fifteens.

But in the end the weather interfered with Luma's plan. Heavy thunderstorms rolled into Atlanta early in the week, soaking the field. The rain trailed off on Wednesday night. The scrimmage was on. So on Thursday afternoon, the Thirteens and Fifteens gathered at Milam Park. The air was cool and damp. The wet grass clung to the ball like glue.

"You play this game like it's a real game," Luma told the Thirteens. "No clowning around. No joking around. No switching up your positions when you feel like it."

Luma left the Under Fifteens to coach themselves. Kanue, Natnael, and Muamer took charge. They understood that their pride was on the line. They hadn't had a successful season, but they still weren't about to lose to the younger team. The Thirteens had something to prove too. Some of the boys, like Bien and Eldin, had older brothers on the Fifteens. But even the younger boys who didn't have relatives wanted to earn the older boys' respect.

Luma blew the whistle, and the game began. Right away, the Thirteens showed they had come to play. They fought the older boys for loose balls, made crisp passes, and managed one run after another against the Fifteens' goal. And yet they kept missing their shots. By the end of the first half, the Thirteens had taken eight shots on goal and missed all of them. The Fifteens, badly outplayed by the younger boys, held the lead, 1–0.

Luma summoned the Under Thirteens over to a corner of the field. She told the younger boys that they were trying to show off. She wanted them to calm down and to aim their shots. She wanted her defense to move up the field and to stay even with one another, in order to draw the offside calls on the faster competition. And she wanted the Thirteens to keep the pressure on.

The Fifteens, meanwhile, were angry. Even though they led by a goal, they knew they were being embarrassed by the younger team. They'd lost their last game of the season, and the idea of losing to the Thirteens was more than they could bear. So when Luma blew the whistle to start the second half, the Fifteens came out attacking. But the Thirteens held fast. Eventually, the Fifteens began to wear down the younger boys and to find the seams in the Thirteens' defense. Muamer scored on a touch shot from just in front of the goal. And though the Thirteens managed to move the ball down the pitch, they continued to miss.

In the end, the Fifteens won the scrimmage 3–1, but not before the Thirteens managed a final blow to the older boys' pride. It came near the end of the game, as Muamer was chasing down a ball near the touchline, alongside a puddle that ran the length of the field just beyond the boundary. Muamer controlled the ball and tried to make a move down the sideline as the Thirteens' defenders moved in. Muamer misplayed the ball and tumbled out of bounds, face-first in the murky puddle. He looked helplessly at Luma, hoping she'd call a foul. But she waved it off; the tackle was clean, and to the delight of the Thirteens, now bent over in hysterics, Muamer decidedly wasn't.

"If the Under Thirteens win this weekend, they have you to thank," Luma told the Fifteens after the game. "You taught them to be a bit more aggressive, and that was something they hadn't been doing all season."

She turned to the Thirteens.

"The way you guys fought for the ball today, the way when one of them got the ball four of you charged him, that's what you need to do on Saturday," she said. "And none of you quit the entire game. I didn't see any of you walking.

"It was an okay scrimmage," she told the boys before sending them home. The Fugees understood it as high praise.

On Saturday morning the Fugees arrived at the Gwinnett YMCA in their white bus. The boys unloaded and made their way toward the playing fields. They were confident, and on their way to the assigned field they made fun of the competition—decked out with matching gear bags and all those silly-looking parents perched on the sidelines. Today, they were sure, would be their day.

In their first of two games on Saturday, the Fugees would face a familiar opponent: Blue Springs Liberty Fire, the team the Fugees had beaten in a 3–2 comeback earlier in the season. Luma viewed that victory as the turning point of the Under Thirteens' season, the game in which they found confidence and a sense of team identity. The game had also pushed the Fugees into third place in the league's final rankings, one point ahead of none other than the Blue Springs Liberty Fire themselves. Blue Springs wanted revenge.

Luma was anxious. Her team was playing better now than at any point in the season, but she was worried about their shooting. Before the game, Luma had the Fugees line up and take simple shots from directly in front of the net. She wanted them to get a feel for scoring. And yet the balls sailed high over the bar and clunked against the posts. The referee blew his whistle. Practice was over. It was time to play.

"I want to have a hard time picking out MVPs today," Luma told the boys. "I want to see your best game, and I know what your best game looks like, each and every single one of you. I want to kick some major butt today. I want to have some fun. I've been excited about this all week."

"Me too," the boys responded, nearly in unison.

"Let's go," said Luma.

The Fugees played the first ten minutes on Blue Springs's side of the field. Early on, Josiah fired a shot from the top left of the box, which sailed high. Moments later, Jeremiah booted a corner kick across the face of the goal, but there was no one in the middle to finish. The early minutes of the game felt like the scrimmage days before against the Under Fifteens; the Fugees were outplaying the competition but were unable to score.

"Time to get physical!" one of the Blue Springs dads shouted from the sideline.

The Blue Springs players, particularly the midfielders and forwards, were bigger than the Fugees, especially little Qendrim, Mohammed, and Prince. Qendrim, though, wasn't intimidated. He was confidently directing his team from center midfield, ordering defense to move up the field in an effort to set up the offside trap. The timing was perfect: a Blue Springs midfielder booted the ball over the Fugees defense, and to an apparently offside forward. But the linesman didn't raise his flag. The Blue Springs player, unchallenged, dribbled toward Mafoday, who stood in goal, waiting for the shot. When it came—high and toward the middle of the goal— Mafoday raised his arms over his head and tried to jump. The ball sailed just over his fingertips. Blue Springs was up 1–0. Several of the Fugees lowered their heads. They began to play flat, as if convinced that no matter how hard they tried, they would not be able to score. At the half, the Fugees trailed 1–0, and Luma was livid.

"You guys are a pathetic excuse for a soccer team," she told the boys, her voice breaking with anger. "They're beating you to the ball, they're outhustling you, and they're taking more shots. I want to know why that cross that Grace just sent over had nobody to finish it off. Josiah? What was that? All you guys did was talk, talk, talk on the bus. Talk, talk, talk before the game. Making fun of every kid on the field. And look at the way *you're* playing. Stupid! And the thing is, you beat this team already! So you think you're better than them. And you're playing like you think you're better than them. But the fact is, they're better than you. Because they don't want to go home today losing. And it looks to me like I've got players who know how to talk and don't know how to play.

"I've been waiting to see you guys play your best and I haven't seen it," Luma said. "It had better happen in this half."

The Fugees took the field in silence and traded guilty looks as they waited for the referee. When play began, they seemed more focused. Qendrim sent passes to Josiah and Jeremiah on the wings. The Fugees attacked once, then again. Ten minutes into the second half, Josiah tapped the ball past his defender on the left wing and then ran after it, leaving the Blue Springs player frozen behind him. Alone now, he dribbled toward the goal. He tapped the ball to his left: a gentle shot that rolled into the net. The game was tied, 1–1. The Fugees kept fighting, firing a series of quick shots from around the perimeter of the box. Midway through the half, the Fugees had taken seven shots and Blue Springs none, and yet the score was still tied. Qendrim ordered his defense to move farther up the field; he wanted to keep the pressure on.

"Come on, guys," he said. "We gotta win. We gotta get one more."

The Fugees now had a corner kick. Bien floated the ball toward the center of the field, but a Blue Springs player volleyed it back toward him and out of bounds. Quickly, Bien heaved the ball back into play. Jeremiah controlled the throw-in and tapped it back to Bien, who crossed the ball back into the middle and right at Idwar Dikori. Idwar extended his leg and the ball ricocheted off his instep and into the back of the net. The Fugees were ahead 2–1. A few minutes later, Jeremiah added another with a cannon shot from fifteen yards out. His teammates responded by getting on the ground and kissing his shooting foot. When the final whistle blew, the Fugees had won 3–1.

"You played a first half that sucked so bad, I just wanted to make you run laps all season," Luma told them afterward. "To come back and play a second half like that . . . I can't handle it, okay? I almost had a heart attack."

The boys responded with applause. The Fugees had played their best half of soccer yet. The comeback, though, had come at a cost. Qendrim had twisted his ankle and was now limping badly. Shahir, the left midfielder who frequently set up Josiah for attacks down the left sideline, had lost the nails of both his big toes because his cleats had been too tight. He was growing quickly and hadn't been able to afford new shoes. And after a frantic and relentless second half, the Fugees were tired. Luma moved the team to the shade, handed out bananas and snack bars, and encouraged them to drink water. They wouldn't have much time to recover. Their next game at the Tornado Cup started in less than an hour.

In their second game of the day, it took the Fugees' opponents just forty-eight seconds to score—on a long pass down the left side and a quick shot that surprised Mafoday and slipped through his hands. A short while later, their

opponents—a team from Warner Robins, Georgia, called the
Strikers—scored again, this time on Eldin. The Fugees were
getting manhandled. Shahir, already limping, caught an el-
bow to the face and came out with a bloody lip. Later, Grace
was elbowed in the midsection and crumpled over. The Fugees didn't give up. Josiah scored early in the second half,
dancing around the keeper, who had come out of the goal to
challenge him. But as time wound down, the Fugees still
trailed 2–1. In the final moments, Jeremiah fired a shot from
ten yards out. The Strikers' keeper bobbled the ball and
seemed to stumble back into the goal. But the linesman ruled
that the ball had not completely crossed the end line. The
Fugees were spent. They failed to mount another attack. Less
than three hours after their best soccer of the season, they
were beaten 2–1.

The Fugees were scheduled to play a morning game on Sunday, but Luma didn't have high hopes. A single loss, she assumed, would knock the Fugees out of contention for the
cup. To be sure, she'd have to wait for results from the other
afternoon games. For now, Luma had other things to worry
about. She had arranged for a Saturday-night team sleepover
at the YMCA, and she had to get her team fed and rested.
The boys brought blankets and sleeping bags and arranged
themselves on yoga mats around a TV in an upstairs room at
the Y. Luma put on a video of old World Cup highlights and
the movie *Goal!* Despite the excitement of a rare overnight
gathering, the boys dropped off to sleep one by one. Luma
logged on to the Tornado Cup website to check the stand-
ings. The Fugees, she learned, were still in it. If they won

their next game against the Concorde Fire, they were going to the finals.

The Concorde Fire were, in almost every way, the opposite of the Fugees. The team came from one of the Atlanta area's most expensive soccer academies, the Concorde Football Club, in the upscale suburb of Alpharetta.

The Fugees needed an outright win to advance; a tie or a loss would send them home. Luma gathered the Fugees before warm-ups to make sure they understood.

"Play to the whistle," she told them. "If the ref makes a bad call, you keep playing. Okay? You focus on the game and how you're going to win it. Because if you don't, we're going to lose your last game of the season, and you're going home early. And you'll go home to your parents, and you're going to tell them you lost. You'll go home to your brothers and sisters, and you're going to tell them you lost."

Luma narrowed her eyes.

"I'm not going home telling anyone I lost," she said.

Luma ran through the game plan. From watching the Fire warm up, she had already determined that their biggest threat was number 26—Jorge Pinzon. She wanted Grace to mark him and stay with him the whole game. The Fugees defense would play upfield, to try to pull the Fire offside. Qendrim would dole out passes to Jeremiah and Josiah, and she expected them to shoot—a lot.

Just before the whistle, some of the Fugees looked toward the sideline and saw a strange sight. A teacher from Josiah's school had come to see him play. Some older refugee kids from the complexes in Clarkston had managed rides to the game, an hour away from Clarkston, and several volunteers from resettlement agencies showed up as well. For the first time all year, the Fugees had fans.

The Fugees came out shooting. Shahir, the Fugees midfielder, blasted a shot that hit the left post and went wide. Josiah missed another, high. The Fugees had other opportunities—two free kicks and a handful of corner kicks— but time and again the plays were broken up by number 26, Jorge Pinzon. He was fast and amazingly determined. He fought for every ball, and didn't hesitate to put his body at risk if he thought he could gain an advantage. He and Grace leaped in the air to control a high ball, and their skulls collided with a gruesome thud. Grace collapsed to the ground. But Jorge shook off the pain and kept playing.

The Fugees, though, kept attacking. Their passes were sharp and controlled. With eight minutes left in the half and the score still tied at zero, Jeremiah Ziaty carved his way through the Fire defense at the top of the box. He pivoted and turned, and with his left and weaker foot, kicked a line drive that curved down just under the Fire goalie's hands. It was a goal score. At the half, the Fugees led 1–0.

Luma hurried her players into a huddle and began to tick through the adjustments she wanted. She reminded the boys that a one-goal lead was not enough. They needed two more, she said, and reminded them of the stakes.

"You got thirty more minutes—thirty more minutes to decide if this is your last game or not," she told them. "I can't do it."

And there was one more adjustment. She wanted Robin Dikori, the Sudanese speedster, to take over Grace's role in marking Jorge Pinzon.

"Robin, number twenty-six is yours," she said. "I don't want him touching that ball."

In the second half, the Fugees let loose with another fusillade of shots—and misses. It was as if there were some sort of force field in front of the Fire's goal, deflecting the Fugees' shots. Midway through the half, a Fire forward got behind the Fugees defense and began to charge the Fugees' goal. Eldin, alone now at keeper, seemed unsure of what to do. He stood beneath the crossbar, waiting for the shot. When it finally came, Eldin froze, and the ball sailed past him, clean: goal.

The Fugees, though, weren't finished. They immediately charged down the field with a quick sequence of crisp passes through the heart of the Fire's defense. Jeremiah again found himself with a clear shot, this time with his right foot. The ball sailed just high. The Fugees had now missed four shots in the second half alone. The Fire responded with an attack of their own. Again, the left forward for the Fire snuck in behind the Fugees defense and began to charge toward the goal. This time, Eldin came out to challenge. Hurried, the Fire player booted the shot, but the ball flew wildly off course. Then, with fifteen minutes to go in the game, Josiah controlled a loose ball on the left side of the Fire's goal. He tapped a pass to Jeremiah at the top of the box, and Jeremiah charged the goal at a full sprint. He took five steps and fired a shot just over the goalie's head. The Fugees led again, 2–1.

The final minutes of the game were thrilling. By now the other morning games had finished, and as word of the stakes in the Fugees-Fire matchup spread around the complex, the parents and players of other teams had gathered on the slight rise alongside the field to watch and cheer. The boys in gold—the team from Warner Robins, Georgia, who would advance if the Fugees lost their lead—pleaded with the Fire to score one more. But there were others who'd wandered toward the set of bleachers where the Fugees' fans had gathered. With help from the older boys who'd come to watch the Thirteens play, they quickly learned a few of the Fugees' names, and as the Fugees fought to keep their season alive, they heard their names called out by strangers.

"Let's go, Josiah!"

"Nice pass, Bien!"

"Shoot, Jeremiah, shoot!"

In the final minutes of the game, the Fire scrambled to get some kind of shot, but they couldn't find an opening. Prince cleared one ball, Shahir another. Robin was doing his job on defense in shutting down Jorge. During a lull when the ball rolled out of bounds, Qendrim called the defense for a quick talk in front of the Fugees' goal. Eldin, Prince, Robin, and Mohammed put their heads together with him, discussing how they were going to keep the Fire from scoring.

The final minutes of the game were chaotic. Spectators were shouting now, and the boys on both the Fire and the Fugees were calling out instructions to one another. As the clock ticked toward zero, neither could find enough time or open space to take a clean shot. Then Jorge Pinzon of the Fire got free from Robin, about twenty-five yards from the Fugees' goal. Mohammed, Prince, and Qendrim converged, and Robin sprinted to catch up. Pinzon must have sensed that he had little time. He squared his shoulders and leaned his body into the shot, which arced beautifully over the players' heads. Eldin leaped into the air. The ball brushed his hands and deflected just under the bar to tie the game 2–2.

When the final whistle blew a few moments later, the team on the sideline erupted in cheers. They were advancing to the finals. The Fugees' season was over.

"You had 'em," Luma told the boys after the game. "You had 'em at two to one, and you wouldn't finish it.

"You deserved to lose," she continued. "You didn't play your best."

The Fugees gathered their gear sadly. Mafoday Jawneh gazed out at the empty field.

"We lost, I mean, we tied our game," he said. "It was so—" Mafoday interrupted himself and his eyes dropped to the ground.

"I don't know what it was," he said.

The holidays were a festive time in Clarkston. The boys got a break from school, and since few had anywhere to go, they passed the time in one another's apartments, playing video games and hanging out. Luma and Tracy baked cookies and dropped them off for Mayor Swaney at City Hall with a card bearing a photo of the Fugees—a gesture of thanks for letting them use Armistead Field. A few days before Christmas, Santa Claus came by helicopter to Clarkston City Hall. Mayor Swaney was there to greet him, and in the crowd of kids who'd gathered, some of the Fugees milled about and took in the odd sight of a man with a white beard and red suit who traveled by chopper.

The Fugees also had work to do. Luma had told them she would enter the Under Thirteens and Under Fifteens in a big tournament to be held in Savannah in January, on the condition that the boys raised the one thousand dollars necessary for travel and lodging. She helped them organize car washes in the parking lot of the YMCA, but the boys had come up $130 short of their goal. Luma held fast. If they didn't have the money, she said, they weren't going. When someone suggested they ask their parents for the money, Luma told the boys that any player who asked a parent for tournament money would be kicked off the Fugees.

"You need to ask yourselves what you need to do for your team," she told them.

"You need to ask yourself what you need to do for your team," Jeremiah said. He was on the phone with one of his teammates, spreading the word about a team project. The boys were going to rake leaves to make that extra $130. The boys figured they could knock on doors in town and offer their services. There was no need to tell Coach about their plan, unless they raised enough cash. Some of the older boys had agreed to help out. It was time to get to work.

In the evening, Luma's cell phone rang. It was Eldin. He wanted to know if she could pick up Grace and take him home. They'd been raking leaves all day, and he was too tired to walk the two miles up the road to his apartment complex. And oh yeah, Eldin said, he wanted to give her the money.

"What money?" Luma asked.

"You said we needed a hundred and thirty dollars," he told her. "So we've got a hundred and thirty dollars."

* * *

Luma spent Christmas visiting her players' families and delivering boxes of food. The day after Christmas, Luma received a fax on the Town of Clarkston's letterhead. The letter, dated December 26, was addressed to the "Fugees Soccer Team."

Dear Coaching Staff (Luma Mufleh and Tracy Ediger):

This letter is to serve immediate notice that the activity/ball fields located at Milam Park and Armistead Field will no longer be available due to the cities [sic] reactivation of its youth recreation program that will be administered through a local organization. We sincerely hope that the time allotted for the teams [sic] practice was useful and productive for the coaching staff and the players alike.

Luma was stunned. The city council had voted unanimously to grant the Fugees six months' use of the field in October—three months before. Luma called Mayor Swaney at City Hall, but he wouldn't take or return her call.

It didn't take much in the way of probing to discover that the letter—signed by a city official named M. W. Shipman but authorized, as the mayor would later admit, by Mayor Lee Swaney himself—was as full of holes as the mayor's earlier attempts to keep soccer out of the town park. The mayor had no authority to go against the city council's vote to let the Fugees use the field for six months. Even further, no one on the city council seemed to know anything about the "reactivation" of the Clarkston youth sports program. When pressed, the mayor wasn't willing to get into specifics. Later, he would change his story entirely. He explained that he had seen some

adult refugees playing soccer in the park and had assumed
they were affiliated with the Fugees. He had kicked the Fugees out of the park, the story now went, for breaking the
terms of its agreement with the city. But that argument didn't
hold up either. The Fugees had no affiliation with any adult
soccer players. For reasons only he knew, Lee Swaney just
didn't want refugees playing soccer in Milam Park.

In the meantime, Luma had a tournament to prepare for,
and she needed a place to practice. That evening, she logged
on to Google Earth once again and scanned satellite images
of Clarkston. There it was: a small southern town, cut through
by railroad tracks and next to the river of concrete that was
I-285. You could easily make out all those apartment
complexes—shadowed squares and rectangles around half-
empty ponds of asphalt. There were a few green patches visible from the sky. Luma knew them well: the fields at the
community center and in Milam Park. Those were off-limits,
of course. The field behind Indian Creek Elementary leaped
off the screen—a glowing white bowl of chalk that from
above looked like some sort of quarry. And that was about it.
Amid the gas stations, strip malls, fast-food joints, and the
tangle of roads and highways, open space in Clarkston was
hard to find. Pull back the view and Atlanta seemed to swal-
low the little town. There was plenty of open space in the
city's big parks and in the suburbs, outside of Clarkston—
and out of reach for the Fugees. That was frustrating. Pull
back farther, and you got a sense of where Clarkston sat in
America—tucked in a green corner of the country beneath
the gray ridges of the Blue Ridge Mountains. Pull back again,
and the blue oceans came into view, then other continents

and countries—Congo, Sudan, Afghanistan, and Iraq—all looking deceptively calm. Pull back farther still and the curved horizons of the planet revealed themselves—a beautiful ball of green, white, blue, slate, and brown. Someday, somewhere down there, the Fugees would find a home.

EPILOGUE

In the months following the Fugees' 2006 season, a number of problems seemed to shrink, or at least become more manageable.

Paula Balegamire, Grace's mother, learned in a cell phone call from Kinshasa that her husband, Joseph, had not been injured in the riot at Makala after all. Some months later, Joseph was free. He promptly left Congo—which has recently descended once again into civil war—and hopes to reunite with his family, either in the United States or in Europe.

Mandela and Luma made up. The reconciliation took place gradually, rather than at any sort of intense heart-to-heart meeting. Jeremiah, Mandela's younger brother, began to call Luma after the Under Fifteen games to ask about the scores. Jeremiah had never shown much interest in the outcomes of the older boys' games, so Luma rightly deduced that Mandela was putting his younger brother up to the calls. Mandela wanted to know how his former team and his ex-teammates were doing.

As tough as Luma could be, she didn't hold grudges. That wasn't her way. She started talking to Mandela again, advising him. She told him she thought it would be a good idea to get away from Clarkston and from Prince and some of his other friends who were dropping out of school. She suggested he apply to Job Corps, a U.S. government program that provides vocational training to people between the ages of sixteen and twenty-four and that offers the chance to earn a high school degree. There was a Job Corps program in Kentucky, she said, far away from the bad crowd in Clarkston. Luma dropped off an application at the Ziatys' apartment and told Mandela that if he wanted to go, he'd have to fill out the application himself.

A few weeks passed before Mandela called. He'd filled out the paperwork. He wanted to go. Mandela was accepted, and soon shipped out to Kentucky. He studied construction and graduated in November 2008 with his high school diploma.

There were other academic success stories among the 2006 Fugees. Shamsoun, Natnael, and Yousph were all accepted at Pfeiffer University, a liberal arts college in North Carolina. Shamsoun received a scholarship to play soccer at Pfeiffer. Since enrolling, he has been working with a pastor from his village in the Nuba Mountains to start a school for Moro children. With the help of family and friends in the Sudanese community, Shamsoun raised more than two thousand dollars so he could attend the inauguration of President

Barack Obama with a student group. Shahir Anwar, of the Under Thirteen Fugees, was accepted at Paideia School, a private school in an affluent Atlanta neighborhood, on scholarship. Many of the Fugees have seen their grades improve as they have become more familiar with English and have taken advantage of the program's tutoring sessions.

But there are still challenges. Kids fall away or get dropped from the program if they don't meet academic expectations. And the local public schools continue to fail the refugee population—and American students as well. The angriest I think I ever saw Luma was when one of her young players proudly showed her his report card, which revealed an A in English. From tutoring sessions, Luma knew the boy was almost completely illiterate.

There have been departures—from the program and from Clarkston. For many refugee families, Clarkston is just a first stop in America, a place to get a foothold before moving on to secondary migration centers in the United States. Liberians, for example, often moved to Iowa; Somalis to Minneapolis or Lewiston, Maine; and Sudanese to Omaha, Nebraska, to seek out the support of communities of family, friends, and countrymen. In the summer of 2007, Beatrice Ziaty decided to leave Clarkston for Iowa, taking young Jeremiah with her while Mandela was in Job Corps in Kentucky. Generose decided to move her three boys, Alex, Bienvenue, and Ive, and her little girl, Alyah, to Fort Wayne, Indiana, a place, she had heard, where life was quieter and safer than in Atlanta. Kanue Biah decided to try out for the Silverbacks, the elite Atlanta soccer club, and made the team, while

Qendrim left the Fugees because he could no longer get rides to and from Clarkston from his family's apartment outside town. Luma tried to cope with the departures as best she could.

In their new homes, the families Luma worked with are once again settling into new lives. Moves can be difficult for everyone, but especially for these refugee children, who were just getting used to life in Atlanta. In the case of eight-year-old Ive, however, his family's move to Indiana wasn't as hard as he had feared it might be. "Hey, guess what?" Ive said excitedly by phone soon after his family had arrived in Fort Wayne.

"I don't know—what?" I said.

"Indiana," Ive declared, "is *in America*."

"I know—it's in the Midwest."

"Well, I thought we were moving to a *totally different country*!" Ive said. For weeks after Generose told her boys that they were moving to Indiana, Ive had believed he would have to learn a new language and new customs when he got there, as he had when he'd moved to America in the first place. But in Indiana, people spoke English. They ate pizza. You could watch *The Simpsons* on TV. Ive was relieved.

Generose works as a cleaning attendant at a hospital in Fort Wayne. The boys are doing well in school and, of course, are playing soccer. Bien broke his middle-school's scoring record his first year in Indiana, with nineteen goals. Like many of the boys who've come and gone through the Fugees, they stay in touch with their old coach, and even took a Greyhound bus to Georgia one summer to spend a week at Luma's house.

To deal with these separations, Luma has learned to turn her attention to other kids in need in Clarkston. A steady flow of refugees into town—most recently, Burundians and Karen, a persecuted ethnic group from Burma—has meant that there has been no shortage of boys who want to try out for the Fugees. "The minute some kid leaves our team you have five more kids who want to take his place," Luma said. "And they're all just as beautiful and innocent or messed up as the kid before them. So you can't stop."

In January 2007, the *New York Times* ran a front-page story I'd written about the Fugees, one of three articles about Clarkston that I wrote for the paper while working on this book. The article, which detailed Mayor Swaney's ban on soccer in the town park, prompted an unexpected response. Mayor Swaney was deluged with angry phone calls and emails from *Times* readers who were appalled that he had kicked the Fugees out of the town park after Christmas.

As the mayor scrambled to explain and reexplain himself in the wake of the public outcry, the City Council of Clarkston took up the matter once again and reaffirmed the Fugees' right to use the field through the spring. The *Times* article about the Fugees also changed things for the team in other ways. The newspaper's readers donated to the Fugees in amounts large and small, and a deal was made for film rights to the Fugees' story. The donations—which included a bus—allowed Luma to end her relationship with the YMCA. Nike stepped in to provide equipment and uniforms. Since then Luma has been free to run her program the way she sees fit, and to fund-raise toward her real ambition: building a tutoring center and soccer facility within walking distance of

Clarkston. Already, Luma has hired two teachers to work with her players. Twelve members of the team now attend classes full-time at the Fugees Academy.

The media attention brought other results. At the tournament in Savannah that the Fugees had raked leaves to attend, for example, locals who'd read about the team came to watch them play and to cheer them on. To his surprise and utter delight, Qendrim was asked to give his first autograph—to a young boy who'd turned out to see the Fugees play. Volunteers have reached out to the program; the Fugees currently have seven interns who help with logistics. The extra help has freed Luma to focus her energies on her real love: coaching.

Relations between the City of Clarkston and the Fugees, for the most part, have improved. Every so often, Luma has to go back to ask to extend the team's use of the field in Milam Park, and so far, the council has always agreed. As for Mayor Swaney, his term ended in 2009. Luma still gives fiery halftime speeches, and admits she had a hard time controlling herself when one of her teams recently blew a 5–1 second-half lead. In the months after the *Times* story about the Fugees, Luma was frequently approached by teachers, parents, coaches, and volunteers who wanted her advice on how to handle various situations involving difficult children. Luma was reluctant to give advice. She doesn't believe in any single method for dealing with struggling kids, and freely admits that the Fugees hasn't worked for everyone. "You're not going to be able to do everything for all the kids," she said. "There's not a perfect system. There's nothing wrong with another way of doing it."

I once asked Tracy Ediger, the Fugees' team manager and all-around helper to the players and their families, what she thought people most misunderstood about Luma and the Fugees program. She didn't hesitate with her response: it was the tendency of people to assume that she and Luma must be saints. "Putting Luma on a pedestal is counterproductive," she wrote me once in an email. "Luma is really a normal person doing what she can for the people around her. If people can look at her and see that, that she's human, not a saint or a superhero, and that she doesn't—can't—do everything or effect miracles, then maybe they can say to themselves, 'I need to look around myself and see my neighborhood, and what is going on here and five streets over, and what I can do in terms of investing myself and my time, to be present for the people around me, and to do something positive for change in my community.'

"No one person can do everything," Tracy said. "But we can all do something."

Since the season written about in *Outcasts United*, Coach Luma has continued to expand her programs for the Fugees in amazing ways. She has started a full-time school, the Fugees Academy, which now serves more than thirty refugee students. The Fugees Family, the nonprofit organization Coach Luma started to support her programs, bought eighteen acres of property just outside Clarkston that will someday serve as the home to the Fugees school and soccer teams. Coach Luma has started a girls' team, and she and her program have helped a number of her former players get into college, many of them on scholarships. The Fugees continue to thrive, helped largely by small donors who have decided to get involved and to help Coach Luma's work.

FOR MORE INFORMATION

To learn more about the Fugees, and for ideas on ways to help or get involved, please visit

FugeesFamily.org

or write to

Fugees Family
P.O. Box 388
Scottsdale, GA 30079-0388

For more about the book, including guides for book clubs and educators, visit

OutcastsUnited.com

ABOUT THE AUTHOR

Warren St. John has written for the *New York Observer*, the *New Yorker*, *Wired*, and *Slate*, in addition to his work as a reporter for the *New York Times*. This work is based on his adult title, *Outcasts United: An American Town, A Refugee Team, and One Woman's Quest to Make a Difference*, which has been selected as a common freshman read at over forty colleges and universities. He is also the author of *Rammer Jammer Yellow Hammer: A Journey into the Heart of Fan Mania*, which was named one of *Sports Illustrated*'s best books of the year. St. John was born in Birmingham, Alabama. He lives in New York City with his wife and daughter.